Introduction

Congratulations for making this investment in your marriage!

We are thrilled that you and your spouse have decided to Stop The Foolishness and you both are ready to follow this guide to a healthy marriage. This workbook further unpacks the concepts in our books, Stop The Foolishness for Wives and Stop The Foolishness for Husbands. We have received countless testimonies from husbands and wives regarding the simplicity and practical nature of the books. Many marriages have been restored as a result of wives and husbands intentionally following the guidelines provided in our books.

We have designed this workbook for both of you to grow together in marriage. Our prayer is that the exercises in this workbook will bring you closer, heal hurts and help you have a marriage that will positively impact generations to come.

We would love to stay connected with you!

Email:	hello@paulandfiona.org
Instagram:	@fionaarthurs
	@ paul.arthurs
Facebook:	Paul and Fiona Arthurs
	Wifelife with Fiona (Private Group)
YouTube:	Paul&Fiona
Website:	www.paulandfiona.org

Table of Contents

Part 1

CHAPTER 1 ~ OUR ROLES

CHAPTER 2 ~ OUR EXPECTATIONS

CHAPTER 3 ~ OUR OPEN COMMUNICATION

CHAPTER 4 ~ OUR PRAYER LIFE

Part 2

CHAPTER 5 ~ OUR FINANCES

CHAPTER 6 ~ OUR FAMILY LIFE

CHAPTER 7 ~ OUR INTIMACY

Final Assignments

PART 1

OBJECTIVES

The purpose of Part 1 is two-fold: 1) to help you further unpack the concepts discussed in *Stop the Foolishness for Husbands* and *Stop the Foolishness for Wives* and 2) to establish a strong, healthy foundation for your marriage through your roles, expectations, communication, and prayer life.

We want you to go deeper into self-examination so you can become the best version of yourselves for your marriage. As a couple, you will evaluate and assess where you are individually and relationally in your marriages by completing exercises that cover the following objectives:

- Understand the foundations for a solid marriage
- Understand the power of prayer
- Discover ways to have more open communication
- Recognize healthy perceptions of your roles as husband and wife
- Create expectations that support your marital foundation
- Maintain the health of your marriage
- Identify and eliminate small, destructive patterns
- Foster intimacy and patience
- Understand different needs and perspectives for each other
- Honor each other
- Rebuild and repair relationships
- Reignite passion (especially for those who have been married a long time)
- Take responsibility for the positive and negative contributions to the relationship
- Identify and implement healthy patterns
- Devise action steps and develop strategies to strengthen your marriage
- Create a mission statement and vision for your marriage

OPENING EXERCISE
A Letter to My Best Friend

In this exercise, you will write a letter to your spouse. As you write this letter, reflect on the following questions:

1. What made you fall in love with your spouse?
2. How did you meet?
3. What made you decide that he or she was the right mate for you to marry? Has anything changed since you have been married?
4. How do you feel about him or her now?
5. How have you changed since you have been married? How have your needs or interests changed?
6. How has your spouse changed since you have been married?
7. What do you admire about your spouse?
8. If you have children, what do you like about your spouse's relationship with the kids?

9. Put your guard down and be open. What do you need from your spouse? What makes you happy? What makes you unhappy?
10. What has blocked you from being more intimate or closer to each other?
11. What thoughts do you have about the current state of your relationship?
12. What do you hope to change or improve after going through these exercises?
13. What do you want your relationship to look like in the future?
14. What is your vision for how you want to become the best version of yourself?
15. What is your vision for the best version of your relationship?
16. Include anything else you would like to share with your spouse.
17. Write a prayer for your spouse and seek God for His guidance during this journey through the workbook.

Once you write the letter, you can decide if you want to share it with your spouse. Keep the letter in a special place. After you have completed the workbook, you will reread the letter to see if anything has changed and complete an ending exercise.

Write your letter on the paper provided for you on the next pages.

My Letter to My Husband

My Letter to My Husband

My Letter to My Wife

_____

_____

_____

_____

_____

_____

_____

_____

_____

_____

_____

_____

_____

_____

_____

_____

_____

_____

RELATIONSHIP ICEBREAKERS

As you go through the daily hustle and bustle of life, you may find your focus is more on problems and to-do lists than your spouse. Before you dive deeper into learning how to stop the foolishness in your marriage, you should find out how much you really know about your spouse. These ice breakers are a fun way to engage with each other before starting on the journey of self-discovery and reconnection.

There are six sets of questions below. You may also create questions of your own. You can break the ice in several ways. Here are some suggestions for you:

1) Interview each other.
2) Do a creative version of *The Newlyweds Show*. Write your responses to each question on separate index cards or sheets of white paper. For each question, each of you will take turns guessing and then revealing your answers. Whoever gets the most answers correct must do something special for the winner.
3) Make a short video introduction. We live in a technology-driven society, and videos are being used on online dating sites to introduce people to each other. Date your spouse again. Select one question from each category and record your responses in a video. You are answering the questions about yourself, not your spouse. At the end, tell your spouse one thing that you love about him or her. Give your pitch on why you are still the one for him or her. It could be a romantic act of kindness to encourage your spouse and make his or her day.

Just Funning Around
(Favorite Interests)

- What is your spouse's favorite childhood TV show?

- What is your spouse's ideal travel location?

- What current song does your spouse listen to constantly?

- What movie or book has impacted your spouse the most?

- What does your spouse like to do for fun?

- What makes your spouse laugh?

- What does your spouse do or say to make you laugh?

Relationship Goals

- The way to my spouse's heart is _____.

- One moment when my spouse felt happy about our relationship was_____.

- My spouse's favorite thing to do or place to go is _____.

- In five years, my spouse wants our relationship to look like_____.

- One thing that motivates my spouse to keep working on our relationship is_____.

- One thing that my spouse wishes I would do more of is_____.

Aspirations

- What are your spouse's 5 year goal?

- What is on your spouse's bucket list?

- Where does your spouse see themselves in ten (10) years?

- What is one dream that your spouse wants to make happen?

Work and Outside Relationships

- My spouse has maintained the longest friendship with _____.

- My spouse prefers to spend time_____.

- My spouse's friends at work are _____.

- If my spouse traded places with his or her supervisor for one day, he or she would _____.

- What my spouse loves the most about his or her job is_____.

- What my spouse dislikes the most about his or her job is_____.

- The family member my spouse would like to reconcile with is _____.

All in My Feelings

- When was the last time your spouse was really scared? _____.

- What helps your spouse relax after a long day? _____.

- How does your spouse like to receive affection? _____.

- What makes your spouse consistently happy? _____.

- What makes your spouse feel most secure? _____.

DIAGNOSTIC ASSESSMENT

Directions: Write your answers to the following questions.

1. In your own words, define what a foundation is.

    _____

    _____

    _____

    _____

2. What does a healthy foundation look like in a marriage? List five characteristics below.

    A. _____

    B. _____

    C. _____

    D. _____

    E. _____

3. What does an unhealthy foundation look like in a marriage? List five characteristics below.

    A. _____

    B. _____

    C. _____

    D. _____

    E. _____

4. On a scale of 1-10, with 1 for very unhealthy and 10 for very healthy, how would you rate the current foundation of your marriage?

Very
Unhealthy_____**Very**
Healthy

     1   2   3   4   5   6   7   8   9 10

5. What are you doing to enhance the foundation of your marriage?

    A. _____

    B. _____

    C. _____

    D. _____

    E. _____

6. What can you do to strengthen the foundation of your marriage?

    A. _____

    B. _____

    C. _____

    D. _____

    E. _____

Chapter 1

Our Roles

A role is a position in which a person is expected to fulfill his or her responsibilities. These responsibilities must be done in order and in excellence because each role plays a vital part in the health of an organization. If a person does not have a clear understanding of his or her role, then the quality of work may affect the organization's overall function and structure. To have a clear understanding of the role, the person must know what the expectations of the position are. These expectations are often aligned with the chief executive officer's or CEO's vision. As the CEO, he or she has the vision and creates the blueprint to execute it.

The chief operating officer (COO) is the second-in-command who administratively carries out the vision and builds it from the blueprint. The COO uses wisdom and discernment to delegate people to assist through the performance of their assigned roles. He or she must put aside his or her own perceptions of how the role should be done in order to walk in agreement with the leader's vision. How a person functions in a role affects how an organization functions in the world. If an organization cannot function effectively, it loses its impact on its areas of influence. If it does not have a sound structure, the organization will collapse due to a lack of balance and an unstable foundation.

Pharaoh had a dream that he could not interpret. He did not know that it was a vision for his kingdom. Pharaoh had people whose roles included dream interpretation as one of their responsibilities. Unfortunately, none of them could operate effectively in their position because they could not interpret the dream. The chief butler remembered how Joseph interpreted his dream when he was in prison. He told Pharaoh, and Joseph's accurate interpretation caused Pharaoh to position him as second-in-command.

Pharaoh was the CEO of Egypt, and now Joseph was the COO. The dream was a vision for Egypt to survive in a future famine. Pharaoh entrusted Joseph to carry out the blueprint. Joseph delegated people to fulfill the vision. Everyone worked in his or her assigned roles in order and in excellence. Egypt had enough resources to withstand the seven years of famine.

It is important for a CEO to assess the health and vitality of the organization. He or she must reevaluate the organization's vision, its roles, and its overall structure and performance. The CEO meets with the COO to discuss where they are and where they want to be. They assess what is working and what is not working. The leaders strategize together as they form a plan of action and possibly redefine roles and restructure departments to strengthen the organization. The overall goal is to ensure growth, stability, and continued success.

A marriage is like an organization. The husband and wife have roles in this covenant relationship. God is the spiritual CEO. His managing partner is Jesus as the spiritual COO. Jesus has entrusted the husband to be the earthly CEO of the marriage, and his wife is to be the earthly COO. It is their responsibility to know what their roles are and assess where they are and where they need to be.

Chapter 1 Objectives

- Gain revelation and understanding about your current view of roles
- Understand what covenant, submission, husband and wife roles, and leading and serving in love mean
- Learn about healthy patterns and perspectives regarding your roles as husband and wife
- Encourage open dialogue and improve communication between you and your spouse
- Create a deeper intimacy in your relationship as you discuss how you want your roles to change for the better
- Commit to grow in learning more about your spouse and his or her role in your relationship

Negative Patterns Addressed in This Chapter

- From *Stop the Foolishness for Husbands*
  - Domineering Leadership
  - Domestic Front
  - Are You Dead Yet?

- From *Stop the Foolishness for Wives*
  - I Can Do It Better
  - The Mother Syndrome
  - But I Have Needs, Too
  - Is It All on Me?
  - Stupid Femininity

Exercise #1
Assessing What We Think About Our Roles

Directions: This reflective exercise will assess where you are as a couple when it comes to your marital roles. Take your time as you reflectively and truthfully take inventory of how you envision each other's roles.

Look at the charts below. The focus of the first chart is on the wife's role and the focus of the second chart is on the husband's role. Each of you will complete the first two columns of the chart that pertains to your role. When you finish the two columns, you will share your responses with each other. Then the wife will ask her husband what he thinks her role should be. She will record his response in the last column of her chart. The husband will ask his wife what she thinks his role should be. He will record her response in the last column of his chart.

My Role as a Wife		
My Thoughts on What It Should Be	My Thoughts on What My Responsibilities Should Be	My Husband's Thoughts on What My Role Should Be

My Role as a Husband		
My Thoughts on What It Should Be	**My Thoughts on What My Responsibilities Should Be**	**My Wife's Thoughts on What My Role Should Be**

Your Reflections on the Exercise

Now that you have completed the charts, discuss the following questions:

1. How do you feel about your mate's perceptions about your role?
2. Where did your views of each other's roles match and where did they differ?
3. Discuss the reasons behind your views. From where did they come?
4. Think about the personal examples of marriages that you have seen in your lives before you met.
   a. How are your perceptions of your roles similar or different from theirs?
   b. What do you recall about how your parents or guardians carried out their roles as husbands and wives?
   c. What part did these examples play in your concept of a husband and a wife?

5. Reflect on your discussion and write your thoughts down below.

_____

_____

_____

_____

_____

_____

_____

_____

_____

_____

_____

_____

_____

_____

_____

_____

_____

_____

_____

_____

_____

_____

_____

_____

_____

_____

_____

_____

Exercise #2

Scenario #1: What is a Covenant?

A covenant is a solemnly binding oath or agreement. In the Hebrew language it literally means "to cut" and involves the shedding of blood. Marriage is a covenant relationship and reminds us of the new covenant that God has made with us through the blood of Jesus. It is important for us to understand the marriage relationship is not a contract that seeks to protect the rights of an individual like a prenuptial agreement, but the emphasis of covenant is on the commitment to follow through on the promise.

A covenant is solemn. It's not a causal relationship, a midnight fling or two ships that pass in the night but there is a sacredness to covenant. When a couple is married that day is set apart from every other day, and everything is done to make the day memorable and special. Due to the solemnity of the covenant relationship it is set apart from all other relationships and given priority. Even in the wedding vows when covenant is made a spouse commits to forsake all other relationships in order to protect the covenant.

Covenant is binding. This means it cannot be amended, annulled or modified in any way. In ancient times the breaking of covenant would be associated with the most horrendous curse. The marriage covenant is a lifelong commitment and should only be severed by death. Binding also implies that two parties are involved, the scriptures say that what God has joined together man should not separate (Mark 10:9).

Covenant is an oath. Words must be communicated either verbally or in writing for covenant to be established. With God's covenant, we learn of His promises, His word, and our role in the covenant. The vows made between husband and wife are the sacred oath that binds the two into covenant relationship. A strong marriage is made up of two people who have made promises to each other and are committed to keep their word.

Covenant is an agreement. Marriage is a spiritual agreement between two parties that calls for a coming together into a partnership based on the fulfillment of promises. The Bible says that two cannot walk together unless they agree. There is a relationship that is based on mutual understanding, love and practice. This agreement is also expressed and sealed through sex which is the consummation of the covenant agreement.

Read the following verses and answer the questions below.

And the LORD God said, "It is not good that man should be alone; I will make him a helper comparable to him." And the LORD God caused a deep sleep to fall on Adam, and he slept; and He took one of his ribs and closed up the flesh in its place. Then the rib which the LORD God had taken from man He made into a woman, and He brought her to the man. And Adam said: "This is now bone of my bones and flesh of my flesh; She shall be called Woman, because she was taken out of Man." Therefore, a man shall leave his father and mother and be joined to his wife, and they shall become one flesh. (Genesis 2:18, 21-24 NKJV)

Yet she is your companion and your wife by covenant. But did He not make them one, Having a remnant of the Spirit? And why one? He seeks godly offspring. Therefore, take heed to your spirit. . . (Malachi 2:14-15 NKJV)

Discussion Questions

1. Discuss these two verses. In your discussion, how would you define the roles of the husband and wife?
2. Explain what a covenant is in your own words.
3. What does a helper look like in your marriage?
4. What has been the blueprint of your marriage? How have you built your marriage? What patterns have you established? Think about what you have currently built. Does it match God's desires?
5. How would people be able to identify that you and your spouse are one flesh? What actions, words, or gestures would they notice? What is affecting you in your journey to maintain yourselves as one flesh?
6. In Malachi 2, the verse says to "take heed to your spirit." We have seen in the verses that husband and wife become one flesh. You are connected by more than just a legal marriage certificate. You are connected emotionally, relationally, mentally, and spiritually. You are one spiritual body. Think of your natural bodies. When you eat the wrong things, allow negative thoughts and emotions to take over your minds and hearts, or neglect your devotional time with the Lord, you see and experience the effects. When you allow the destructive patterns to enter your relationship, you experience the effects and wonder how you arrived at this place. Let's take heed to what is in your spirit and relationship. Discuss with each other how the following negative patterns can affect your covenants.

   a. Not owning your own actions
   b. Placing the blame on your spouse
   c. Using your godly influence to manipulate
   d. Not controlling the atmosphere in your home
   e. Believing that it is all on you
   f. Not recognizing that you are your greatest enemy
   g. Thinking highly of yourselves
   h. Projecting your negative feelings on your spouse
   i. Having a negative attitude
   j. Expecting your spouse to fill any voids
   k. Belittling your spouse in private and in public
   l. Treating your spouse like a child
   m. Being concerned with only your needs and not your spouse's needs
   n. Antagonizing your husband
   o. Taking the leadership role away from your husband
   p. Not respecting your husband's leadership

STOP THE FOOLISHNESS FOR COUPLES

q. Seeing your wife as a subordinate and not a partner in building with you
r. Not making your husband feel needed
s. Not dying to self

Exercise #3

Scenario #2: What is Submission? (The Wife's Role)

To submit means to come under the authority of or to follow one's leadership. It involves surrendering and humbling oneself. Submission in your marriage means your support of your husband's leadership. Does it mean that you have no say in your marriage? Does it involve belittling each other or thinking of each other as less than? Does submission deal with power and position or love and serving? Let's examine the "S" word more closely.

What Submission Is

- A Christlike response toward your husband's leadership
- An expression of grace and love toward your husband
- A willingness to allow your husband to fulfill his God-given role as a priest and leader
- A righteous diligence to be your husband's partner and co-builder
- A commitment to have God's heart toward your husband
- A willingness to be humble

What Submission Is Not

- A feeling or position of inferiority or dominance
- Blind obedience
- Subjection to physical, verbal, emotional, or any other type of abuse
- Submission based on whether or not your husband deserves it
- Competition for control

Your Responsibilities in This Role

- To be a helper (Genesis 2:18)
- To respect, reverence, honor, and esteem your husband (Ephesians 5:33)
- To support your husband in his leadership (Ephesians 5:22-23)
- To love your husband unconditionally, selflessly, sacrificially, and responsively (Titus 2:4)

Discussion Questions

1. Take a moment and think about your marriage. What does submission look like in your relationship? How is submission a part of your role as a wife? Discuss these questions with each other.

2. Read the following scriptures and discuss the questions.

   Wives, submit to your own husbands, as to the Lord. For the husband is head of the wife, as also Christ is head of the church; and He is the Savior of the body. Therefore, just as the church is subject to Christ, so *let* the wives *be* to their own husbands in everything. (Ephesians 5:22-24 NKJV)

   Wives, likewise, *be* submissive to your own husbands, that even if some do not obey the word, they, without a word, may be won by the conduct of their wives, when they observe your chaste conduct *accompanied* by fear. Do not let your adornment be *merely* outward—arranging the hair, wearing gold, or putting on *fine* apparel— rather *let it be* the hidden person of the heart, with the incorruptible *beauty* of a gentle and quiet spirit, which is very precious in the sight of God. (1 Peter 3:1-4 NKJV)

   The wise woman builds her house, but the foolish pulls it down with her hands. (Proverbs 14:1 NKJV)

   a. What does it mean to submit as a wife in these verses? Are there specific actions or descriptions that you can pick out from the verses? Are you doing any of these things as a wife now? If so, what does that look like?

   b. How do you build up your house? What actions, behaviors, or words have been tearing it down?

   c. What negative patterns would hinder a wife from submitting to her husband as described in the verses?

   d. Describe what the role of a wife should be.

   e. Discuss what her responsibilities should be based on your description.

   f. How can you become this role and carry out these responsibilities in your relationship?

Exercise #4

Scenario #3: What is Submission? (The Husband's Role)

Read the following scriptures and information. Answer the questions below.

Husbands, love your wives, just as Christ also loved the church and gave Himself for her, that He might sanctify and cleanse her with the washing of water by the word, that He might present her to Himself a glorious church, not having spot or wrinkle or any such thing, but that she should be holy and without blemish. So, husbands ought to love their own wives as their own bodies; he who loves his wife loves himself. For no one ever hated his own flesh, but nourishes and cherishes it, just as the Lord *does* the church. (Ephesians 5:25-29 NKJV)

Husbands, likewise, dwell with *them* with understanding, giving honor to the wife, as to the weaker vessel, and as *being* heirs together of the grace of life, that your prayers may not be hindered. (1 Peter 3:7 NKJV)

Husbands, love your wives and do not be bitter toward them. (Colossians 3:19 NKJV)

What Leadership as a Husband Is

- A calling to work, sacrifice, and serve
- To be the head
- To pray together with your wife
- Include your wife in planning for the future
- Accept spiritual responsibility for your family
- Willing to say "I'm sorry" and "forgive me" to your family
- Seek your wife's input on major financial decisions
- Compliment your wife often
- Aware of your wife's weaknesses, but focus and accentuate her strengths

What Leadership as a Husband Is Not

- To be a dictator
- To be superior
- To be authoritarian
- To dominate
- To give orders and have to be in control
- Makes all the decisions and expect everyone to carry out directives
- Being inflexible even when you are wrong
- Perceives discussion as a threat

- Become defensive when your wife tries to make suggestions or give her own views and thoughts
- Can't stand to be wrong and let your wife be right
- Can't admit when you are wrong
- Loves to point out your wife's flaws and failures as a form of teasing

Your Responsibilities in This Role

- To be the head (Ephesians 5:23-30)
- To provide for your family (1 Timothy 5:8, Proverbs 13:22)
- To protect (1 Peter 3:7)
- To cultivate (Ephesians 5:29)
- To love as Christ loves the Church (Ephesians 5:25-27)

Discussion Questions

1. What does it mean to submit as a husband? Are there specific actions or descriptions that you can pick out from the verses or information? Are you doing any of these things as a husband now? If so, what does that look like?

2. For the husband's role, discuss examples of what submission as a husband is and what it is not.

3. How can you dwell with your wife with understanding? What do you do to nourish and cherish your wife?

4. What negative patterns would hinder a husband from submitting to his wife as described in the verses or information?

5. How can you become this role and carry out these responsibilities in your relationship?

Exercise #5

Scenario #4: Examining Roles in Ahab and Jezebel's Marriage

(1 Kings 21:3-11 NKJV)

Read the following verses and discuss the questions below.

But Naboth said to Ahab, "The LORD forbid that I should give the inheritance of my fathers to you!" So, Ahab went into his house sullen and displeased because of the word which Naboth the Jezreelite had spoken to him; for he had said, "I will not give you the inheritance of my fathers." And he lay down on his bed, and turned away his face, and would eat no food. But Jezebel his wife came to him, and said to him, "Why is your spirit so sullen that you eat no food?" He said to her, "Because I spoke to Naboth the Jezreelite, and said to him, 'Give me your vineyard for money; or else, if it pleases you, I will give you *another* vineyard for it.' And he answered, 'I will not give you my vineyard.'"

Then Jezebel his wife said to him, "You now exercise authority over Israel! Arise, eat food, and let your heart be cheerful; I will give you the vineyard of Naboth the Jezreelite." And she wrote letters in Ahab's name, sealed *them* with his seal, and sent the letters to the elders and the nobles who *were* dwelling in the city with Naboth. She wrote in the letters, saying, "Proclaim a fast, and seat Naboth with high honor among the people; and seat two men, scoundrels, before him to bear witness against him, saying, "You have blasphemed God and the king." *Then* take him out, and stone him, that he may die. So, the men of his city, the elders and nobles who were inhabitants of his city, did as Jezebel had sent to them, as it *was* written in the letters which she had sent to them. (1 Kings 21:3-11)

Discussion Questions

1. How would you describe Ahab's role as a husband in this marriage?
2. How would you describe Jezebel's role as a wife in this marriage?
3. What negative patterns from the books do you notice?
4. Is their marriage covenant aligned with God's vision?
5. What have you learned from these Scriptures that you can apply to your own roles in your marriage?
   a. If there are negative, destructive patterns, what healthy patterns should be in place?
   b. What could Ahab and Jezebel have done differently?
   c. What can you do differently?

Exercise #6

Scenario #5: Examining Roles in Job's Marriage
(Job 2:7-10, 19:17 NKJV)

Read the following verses and discuss the questions below.

So, Satan went out from the presence of the LORD, and struck Job with painful boils from the sole of his foot to the crown of his head. And he took for himself a potsherd with which to scrape himself while he sat in the midst of the ashes. Then his wife said to him, "Do you still hold fast to your integrity? Curse God and die!" But he said to her, "You speak as one of the foolish women speaks. Shall we indeed accept good from God, and shall we not accept adversity?" In all this Job did not sin with his lips. (Job 2:7-10)

My breath is offensive to my wife. (Job 19:17a)

Discussion Questions

1. How would you describe Job's role as a husband in this marriage?
2. How would you describe his wife's role in this marriage?
3. What negative patterns from the books do you notice?
4. Is their marriage covenant aligned with God's vision?
5. What have you learned from these Scriptures that you can apply to your own roles in your marriage?
   a. If there are negative, destructive patterns, what healthy patterns should be in place?
   b. What could Job and his wife have done differently?
   c. What can you do differently?

Exercise #7

Scenario #6: Examining Roles in a 21st Century Marriage

Read the following scenario and discuss the questions below.

Diane* had gotten the mail out of the mailbox and walked into the house. She saw the past due notice from the mortgage company. She became upset at what she read. Lee* hadn't made the last three payments, and the bank was preparing to foreclose. She had been working three jobs now for three months. Diane worked as a full-time university instructor during the day, taught part-time classes online, and worked as a salesperson for Walmart on the weekends.

Before she was hired for these three jobs, Diane wasn't making enough to cover the mortgage payments. In fact, she thought it was her husband's role to pay for the bills and provide for the family as the head of the household. Right now, she was disappointed. She expected him to do his part. She always submitted to his decisions and leadership, trusting him to do the right thing. Well, it seemed like everything was on her now. They had a young daughter who needed a stable home. Plus, Diane's father was never like that. She remembers her father working two jobs and her mother worked as well, but her father always paid the bills. Diane's mom took care of her personal bills. As Diane's father sat down at the table to pay bills, he would ask Diane to join him so he could show her how to budget and to stress that the man's responsibility was to take care of his household. His wife should not lack for anything.

Well, Diane thought to herself that she had to take matters in her own hands. She paid the late payments and assumed the role of paying for the mortgage. Lee got angry at her for stepping in. He told her that she made him feel like less of a man. Lee remembers how his mother had to struggle to take care of him because his father was not around. He wanted to be a better husband and father. Arguments continued, even though Diane relinquished the responsibility of paying the mortgage and gave it back to her husband.

*= fictitious names and situation

Discussion Questions

1. How would you describe Lee's role as a husband in this marriage?
2. How would you describe Diane's role as a wife in this marriage?
3. What negative patterns from the Stop the Foolishness do you notice?
4. Is their marriage covenant aligned with God's vision?
5. What have you learned from these scriptures that you can apply to your own roles in your marriage?
    a. If there are negative, destructive patterns, what healthy patterns should be in place?
    b. What could Lee and Diane have done differently?

    c.   What can you do differently?

Exercise #8
Writing Prompts

Loving Each Other Through Servant Leadership

In John 13:1-14, Jesus illustrated to his disciples what it meant to be a servant leader through an act of compassion and humility. He forgot about His position as their master and teacher. He removed the clothing that signified Him as a leader and put on the clothes that signified a servant, but He still had authority. Jesus served them in love. Your role as a husband and wife involves servant leadership, humility, and most importantly, love. As we have examined destructive patterns in our book, we have shown what happens when we seek our own desires first, assume dominance, put all the responsibility on each other, or become a parent to our spouses. As you have gone through the diagnostic assessments and discussed the scenarios, you have explored what submission, covenant, and roles mean in Biblical and real-life applications.

Now it is time to learn the healthy, divine patterns that comprise your role as a husband and wife. Let's process your thoughts through writing first. Paper is provided on additional pages.

1. Think about how Jesus served with love during His ministry. What can you learn from Him? What actions from His examples of serving and leading in love can you implement in your relationship?

2. As a husband, how can I be a servant to my wife? How can I lead by serving and loving? What would leading my wife and home in service and love look like in our marriage?

3. As a wife, how can I be a servant to my husband? How can I support him, build from his vision, and serve through love? What would serving in love as a wife look like in our marriage?

4. If I accept my role as a husband or wife as one of leading or serving in love, what are three actions or responsibilities that I need to do?

5. Choose one of the items from your list above. Create a plan of action steps to put this action or responsibility into motion now in your relationship. Each action step can be one thing you plan to do daily or weekly.

Reflections

_____

_____

_____

_____

_____

_____

_____

_____

_____

_____

_____

_____

_____

_____

_____

_____

_____

_____

_____

_____

Exercise #9
Is It a Covenant Breaker or Keeper?

Directions: You will see a list of words below. These words are descriptions or actions that can either break or maintain a covenant marriage. After the list of words, you will see a chart with two columns titled "Covenant Breakers" and "Covenant Keepers." With your spouse, complete the chart by deciding where each description or action should go. Afterwards, discuss which ones are present in your relationship, which ones you need to remove, and which ones you need to keep and improve.

You can write your responses in the chart provided. The second option is to make it interactive by cutting out the words and the column title strips and manually placing the words under the appropriate column.

LOVE	BLAME	COMPLAINING
BUILT UP OR UNRESOLVED ANGER	FORGIVENESS	AMBIVALENCE
TAKING RESPONSIBILITY FOR MY OWN ACTIONS	DISSENSION	ARGUING
GOD-SUFFICIENCY	MANIPULATION	SELF-SUFFICIENCY
COMMITMENT	MERCY	SELF-EXAMINATION
COMPASSION	SUBMISSION	CRITICISM
SHAME	APATHY	SERVING
SELFLESSNESS	CONTROLLING	BELITTLING
PRIDE	HUMILITY	MY NEEDS, MY WILL, MY WAY, MY EXPECTATIONS
NEGLECT	ASSUMING ALL RESPONSIBLITIES/OVERLOAD	MOTHERING
BEING A FATHER TO YOUR WIFE	ARROGANCE	WIFE AS THE MAN OF THE HOUSE
UNHEALED WOUNDS	DOMINEERING	APATHY

SUPPORT	WIFE AS THE BUILDER OF MARITAL VISION	HUSBAND AS THE LEADER OF THE MARITAL VISION
OFFENSE	GOODNESS	GENTLENESS
COMMUNICATION	PEACE	JEALOUSY/ENVY
COMPARISON/ PERFECTION	DIVISION	KINDNESS
PATIENCE	STUBBORNNESS	ISOLATION
REJECTION	ABANDONMENT	UNFORGIVENESS
WHAT'S IN IT FOR ME?	WHAT'S IN IT FOR GOD?	WHAT'S IN IT FOR MY SPOUSE?
CHERISHING	NOURISHING	GENEROUS & GRATEFUL HEART
GRACE	BITTERNESS	FAITHFULNESS
SURRENDER	PARTNERSHIP	AGREEMENT

INTERACTIVE STRIPS FOR THE 2ND OPTION

COVENANT BREAKERS	COVENANT KEEPERS

Exercise #10
Putting Concept into Action

Now it is time to put the concept into action. Review your responses to the assessments and exercises for this chapter. Reflect on what you have read in our books. You are going to think about five actions or situations regarding your roles that you want to improve. These actions deal with the destructive, unhealthy patterns that we have written about regarding roles. Once you list those patterns, actions, or situations, you are going to write a Biblical response to them that would involve a healthy, divine pattern. Then you will create action steps to help you implement the healthy patterns. This exercise will be in most of the chapters. You can return to the following example for future exercises.

Example from Discussion Scenario #5:

Destructive Pattern/Thought: I wish my husband was more like my daddy. He needs to act like the head of the household before I do.

Divine Pattern/Thought: In Ephesians 5:31-33, husband and wives leave their fathers and mothers and become one flesh. The husband loves his wife as himself, and the wife should respect her husband. I am still cleaving to my father and he has now become a part of our marital flesh. It is not fair to compare my husband to someone he is not. I am not showing respect. My frustration is with the bills not being paid on time. How can I help my husband deal with the burden of bearing our financial load?

Developing Strategies: I can sit down with my husband at a designated time each month and help him with creating a budget. Since he is the leader, I can have him create the budget, and I can offer suggestions and input. I can tell him how I can help. As the managing partner and builder, I can help build his vision by watching my spending habits, contributing money to our savings account, and selecting some of the bills to contribute with the payments.

Your Turn:

1. **Destructive Patterns/Thoughts:** Oftentimes, we may say to ourselves, "I really wish my spouse would do this," "It really gets on my nerves that he or she does or doesn't do this," "I feel like he or she doesn't understand me or care about my needs when he or she does this." We often have expectations of what our spouse should be and do as a husband or wife. Along with those expectations, we have complaints or disappointments about things he or she should be or shouldn't be doing as a husband or wife. Make a list of those five (5) things.

   A._____

   B._____

   C._____

   D._____

   E._____

2. **Divine Patterns/Thoughts:** What would be the Biblical response to those five (5) things that you have listed? How can you respond in a healthy way?

   A._____
   _____
   _____

   B._____
   _____
   _____

   C._____
   _____
   _____

   D._____
   _____
   _____

   E._____
   _____
   _____

3. **Developing Strategies:** Think of three (3) actions that you can do to incorporate healthy, divine patterns into your relationship regarding this concern.

A._____

        1._____
        2._____
        3._____

B._____

        1._____
        2._____
        3._____

C._____

        1._____
        2._____
        3._____

D._____

        1._____
        2._____
        3._____

E._____

        1._____
        2._____
        3._____

Chapter 1 Writing Reflection
Marital Role Description

A position for an organization will include a description of the role and the responsibilities. Create an advertisement for your ideal role for you and your spouse based on what you have learned. What do you want your role as a husband to look like? What do you want your role as a wife to look like? What would be the responsibilities of each role? Now write them below. You will use this reflection to help you with the last chapter's exercises.

Wife's Reflections

_____

_____

_____

_____

_____

_____

_____

_____

_____

_____

_____

_____

Husband's Reflections

_____

_____

_____

_____

_____

_____

_____

_____

_____

_____

_____

_____

_____

_____

_____

_____

_____

_____

_____

Chapter 2

Our Expectations

An expectation is a positive or negative belief about someone or something. Each expectation builds upon another one until a system of thoughts has been created. This system is a platform on which we set our husbands, wives, and marriages. When an expectation is unmet, the platform becomes uneven and not sturdy. As more expectations fall, the platform that we have single-handedly built is no longer standing. Our expectations of each other and our marriages can become a pedestal if they are unrealistic and unhealthy. That pedestal becomes an impossible ideal that *we* have created for our spouse and marriage. That ideal is now an idol.

When we say that we want to exchange our gift or spouse because we view the 20% as failing our expectations, we tell God that His ideal for the gift is wrong and our ideal is right. Having expectations is not wrong, but unhealthy or negative ones are. Our expectations should be healthy and positive, and we should have open communication about them. We should consult the Lord in prayer about our expectations and spouses because He is the Creator of everyone and everything. He intimately knows what He has created.

Ladders are tools that help us to climb up to the different levels of any building. With each step, we must grab the rung or hold on to each side. If we take more than one step at a time, we risk the chance of losing our footing and experiencing serious injuries. These injuries may call for weeks of recovery. Our loved ones would worry about how they could have lost us because we lacked consideration and wisdom as we advanced to different levels.

With each year of our marriage, we reach different levels in our relationship. Sometimes we forget about our spouse's expectations. Things have become comfortable, and little things are taken for granted. Lack of consideration can lead to frustration, dishonor, and distance. We have stopped making our spouses a priority because we expect them to always be there. If we do not address the unhealthy patterns regarding our expectations, then we may find that they are not there, be it physically, mentally, or emotionally.

The Lord has given us everything that pertains to life and godliness. Healthy patterns for our expectations can be found in the ladder of faith described in 2 Peter 1:3-8. The ladder is set on the great and precious promises and our partaking of the divine nature. The platform is the gift of grace that God gives through salvation and grounds us in our faith. Each rung is a level in our spiritual development. To achieve virtue, knowledge, temperance, patience, godliness, brotherly kindness and charity, we must endure difficult situations. They help us to reach each level in the ladder of faith and produce the fruit of the Holy Spirit.

Our marriages are a part of this upward climb of the ladder. What we label as flaws or unmet expectations are God-designed lessons to help us see the gift of our spouse through God's eyes, heart, and expectations. The ladder of faith is also one for our relational development. The following exercises will challenge unhealthy patterns regarding expectations and show us how to have a healthy spirit of expectation to discover the different levels in our God-given gifts: our spouses.

Chapter 2 Objectives

- Gain revelation and understanding about your current view of expectations
- Understand what grace and honor mean
- Learn about healthy patterns and perspectives regarding your expectations as husband and wife
- Encourage open dialogue and improve communication between you and your spouse
- Create a deeper intimacy in your relationship as you discuss how you want your expectations to change for the better
- Commit to grow in learning more about your spouse and his or her expectations for your marriage

Negative Patterns Addressed in This Chapter

- From *Stop the Foolishness for Husbands*
  - Lack of Consideration – You Didn't Butter My Toast
  - I'm Not Sick—Physical Health

- From *Stop the Foolishness for Wives*
  - Can I Exchange My Gift?

Exercise #1
Assessing What We Think About Our Expectations

Directions: This reflective exercise will assess where you are as a couple when it comes to your expectations. Take your time as you reflectively and truthfully take inventory of what you expect from your marriage and each other. Answer the questions below.

1. **The Ladder of Expectations for Your Marriage:** List 7 expectations that you have for your marriage in the middle column. Next, rank them in order of importance in the first column (Rank#1). When you finish the chapter, you will rank them again in the last column (Rank#2) to see if there are any changes.

Rank#1   Rank#2

____   1. _____   ____

____   2. _____   ____

____   3. _____   ____

____   4. _____   ____

____   5. _____   ____

____   6. _____   ____

____   7. _____   ____

2. **The Ladder of Expectations for Your Spouse:** Now answer the following questions regarding your spouse using the spiritual virtues on the ladder of faith.

For Your Husband

a. What are three expectations that you have for your husband regarding love?

1. _____

2. _____

3. _____

b. What are three expectations that you have for your husband regarding kindness?

1. _____
2. _____
3. _____

c. What are three expectations that you have for your husband regarding Godly living and being the priest of your home?

1. _____
2. _____
3. _____

d. What are three expectations that you have for your husband regarding patience?

1. _____
2. _____
3. _____

e. What are three expectations that you have for your husband regarding self-control?

1. _____
2. _____
3. _____

f. How do you expect your husband to apply his knowledge of the scriptures to his daily living in your marriage?

1. _____
2. _____
3. _____

g. How do you expect your husband to operate in virtue or high moral standards in your marriage and his daily living?

    1. _____

    2. _____

    3. _____

h. How do you expect your husband to exercise his faith in every area of your marriage (finances, children, employment, your relationship, etc.)?

    1. _____

    2. _____

    3. _____

For Your Wife

i. What are three expectations that you have for your wife regarding kindness?

    1. _____

    2. _____

    3. _____

j. What are three expectations that you have for your wife regarding Godly living and being your help meet and builder of your home?

    1. _____

    2. _____

    3. _____

k. What are three expectations that you have for your wife regarding patience?

       1. _____

       2. _____

       3. _____

l. What are three expectations that you have for your wife regarding self-control?

       1. _____

       2. _____

       3. _____

m. How do you expect your wife to apply her knowledge of the scriptures to her daily living in your marriage?

       1. _____

       2. _____

       3. _____

n. How do you expect your wife to operate in virtue or high moral standards in your marriage and her daily living?

       1. _____

       2. _____

       3. _____

o. How do you expect your wife to exercise her faith in every area of your marriage (finances, children, employment, your relationship, etc.)?

       1. _____

       2. _____

       3. _____

Exercise #2

Scenario #1: What is Grace?

Read the following verses and discuss the questions below.

For the gifts and the calling of God are irrevocable [for He does not withdraw what He has given, nor does He change His mind about those to whom He gives His *grace* or to whom He sends His call]. (Romans 11:29 AMP) (Emphasis added)

For it is by grace [God's remarkable compassion and favor drawing you to Christ] that you have been saved [actually delivered from judgment and given eternal life] through faith. And this [salvation] is not of yourselves [not through your own effort], but it is the [undeserved, gracious] gift of God; (Ephesians 2:8 AMP)

Discussion Questions

1. How would you define grace?
2. How do you extend grace to your spouse?
3. How do your expectations of your spouse and marriage show grace?
4. God gave us gifts that He does not take back despite how we do not always meet His expectations. He gives us the gift of salvation through grace despite our sins: Are you following His example with each other when you do not meet your spouse's expectations?
5. What if the irrevocable gift and calling of God is your spouse? What if he or she is a gift and a calling from God given to you to teach you about grace? What have you learned about grace from your relationship with your spouse?
6. What have you learned from these scriptures that you can apply to your expectations of each other?

Exercise #3

Scenario #2: What is Honor?

In the same way, you wives, be submissive to your own husbands [subordinate, not as inferior, but out of <u>respect</u> for the responsibilities entrusted to husbands and their accountability to God, and so partnering with them] so that even if some do not obey the word [of God], they may be won over [to Christ] without discussion by the *godly* lives of their wives, when they see your modest and respectful behavior [together with your devotion and appreciation—love your husband, encourage him, and enjoy him as a blessing from God].

In the same way, you husbands, live with *your wives* in an understanding way [with great gentleness and tact, and with an intelligent regard for the marriage relationship], as with someone physically weaker, since she is a woman. Show her <u>honor *and* respect</u> as a fellow heir of the grace of life, so that your prayers will not be hindered *or* ineffective. (1 Peter 2:1-2, 7 AMP)

Discussion Questions

1. How would you define honor?
2. How do you honor each other?
3. How do you show consideration for each other?
4. How do your expectations show honor toward your spouse?
5. Do any of your expectations show dishonor toward your spouse? If yes, what can you do differently?
6. Discuss times when you have felt respected and when you have felt disrespected. What changes do you need to make?
7. Discuss times when you have felt like a priority in your spouse's life and when you have not felt like a priority. What changes do you need to make?
8. What have you learned from these Scriptures that you can apply to your expectations of each other?

Exercise #4

Scenario #3: Examining Expectations in Jacob, Rachel, and Leah's Marriage (Genesis 29:17-18, 21-25, & 31-35)

Leah's eyes *were* delicate, but Rachel was beautiful of form and appearance. Now Jacob loved Rachel; so, he said, "I will serve you seven years for Rachel your younger daughter."

Then Jacob said to Laban, "Give *me* my wife, for my days are fulfilled, that I may go in to her." And Laban gathered together all the men of the place and made a feast. Now it came to pass in the evening that he took Leah his daughter and brought her to Jacob; and he went in to her. And Laban gave his maid Zilpah to his daughter Leah *as* a maid. So, it came to pass in the morning, that behold, it *was* Leah. And he said to Laban, "What is this you have done to me? Was it not for Rachel that I served you? Why then have you deceived me?"

When the LORD saw that Leah *was* unloved, He opened her womb; but Rachel *was* barren. So, Leah conceived and bore a son, and she called his name Reuben; for she said, "The LORD has surely looked on my affliction. Now therefore, my husband will love me." Then she conceived again and bore a son, and said, "Because the LORD has heard that I *am* unloved, He has therefore given me this *son* also." And she called his name Simeon. She conceived again and bore a son, and said, "Now this time my husband will become attached to me, because I have borne him three sons." Therefore, his name was called Levi. And she conceived again and bore a son, and said, "Now I will praise the LORD." Therefore, she called his name Judah. Then she stopped bearing.

Discussion Questions

1. How would you describe Jacob's expectations of Leah and Rachel? What did the wives expect from him?
2. How did he show grace and honor to Rachel and Leah? How did he show a lack of grace and honor toward his wives? Do you think the wives showed any grace or honor toward Jacob?
3. Who was the source of Leah's life? When did her source change? Who was her new source?
4. What negative patterns from the books do you notice?
5. Who is your source? Do you expect your spouse to fulfill all your needs? Are some of your expectations things that God should fulfill?
6. What have you learned from these Scriptures that you can apply to your own roles in your marriage?
   a. If there are negative, destructive patterns, what healthy patterns should be in place?
   b. What could Jacob and Leah have done differently?
   c. What can you do differently?

Exercise #5

Scenario #4: Examining Expectations in Joseph and Mary's Marriage
(Matthew 1:18-25 AMP)

Now the birth of Jesus Christ was as follows: when His mother Mary had been betrothed to Joseph, before they came together, she was found to be with child by [the power of] the Holy Spirit. And Joseph her [promised] husband, being a just *and* righteous man and not wanting to expose her publicly to shame, planned to send her away *and* divorce her quietly. But after he had considered this, an angel of the Lord appeared to him in a dream, saying, "Joseph, descendant of David, do not be afraid to take Mary as your wife, for the Child who has been conceived in her is of the Holy Spirit. She will give birth to a Son, and you shall name Him Jesus (The LORD is salvation), for He will save His people from their sins." All this happened in order to fulfill what the Lord had spoken through the prophet [Isaiah]: "BEHOLD, THE VIRGIN SHALL BE WITH CHILD AND GIVE BIRTH TO A SON, AND THEY SHALL CALL HIS NAME IMMANUEL"—which, when translated, means, "GOD WITH US." Then Joseph awoke from his sleep and did as the angel of the Lord had commanded him, and he took *Mary* [to his home] as his wife, but he kept her a virgin until she had given birth to a Son [her firstborn child]; and he named Him Jesus (The LORD is salvation).

Discussion Questions

1. How would you describe Joseph's expectations of Mary? How did he show grace and honor toward her?
2. What do you think Mary expected of Joseph?
3. What negative patterns from the books do you notice, or are there healthy patterns here?
4. Who changed his expectations?
5. What kind of gift was Mary to Joseph? How was Joseph a gift to Mary?
6. How is your husband a gift to you? How are you a gift to your wife?
7. Have you ever had something happened in your marriage to make you think twice? Maybe you have said to yourself, "This is not what I signed up for. I did not expect this." What can you learn from Joseph's response and redirection?
8. What have you learned from these Scriptures that you can apply to your expectations?

Exercise #6

Scenario #5: Examining Roles in a 21st Century Marriage

Read the following scenario and discuss the questions below.

Paul* and Raine* were married for ten years. It was his fourth marriage and Raine's first, but Raine didn't know about Paul's previous marriages. He worked two jobs, gambled and drank on Saturday nights, and attended Sunday services with his wife. He married an Alabama girl from the country and thought he had a good, Christian woman. Paul expected his wife to submit to him, cook, and take care of the house. Raine loved everything about Paul. His charismatic personality and North Carolina roots charmed her. She loved their children and her husband with her whole heart. That love overflowed in her diligent service as a hotel maid. One thing that irritated Raine about Paul was his grooming habits. He didn't brush his teeth or shower daily. Paul wore the same clothes over and over. She would buy him clothes and gently told him about his breath and body odor. He always responded in hurt and then lashed out with a few comments of his own. She expected him to maintain good hygiene and take pride in his appearance. She consistently nagged him about it. Then, the unexpected happened. Paul's father visited them one weekend and told her that Paul had seven other children from three previous marriages. Raine was heartbroken. She didn't sign up for this.

*=fictitious names and situation

Discussion Questions

1. How would you describe Paul's expectations of Raine? What did Raine expect for him?
2. How were grace and honor shown or not shown in this marriage?
3. What negative patterns from the books do you notice?
4. What could Paul and Raine have done differently?
5. What would you have done?

Exercise #7
Writing Prompts

It's Time for a Vision Alignment

In Mark 8:22-26, a group of people took a blind man to Jesus and begged for his healing. Jesus walked him away from everyone, spit on his eyes, and laid his hands on them. When he removed his hands from his eyes, he asked the man what he saw. The man stated that he saw men walking like trees. Jesus walked with him a little further and touched him again. Then the man saw every man clearly.

Jesus moved him away from the people. With each walk, he went a little further and aligned his vision. When he reached a certain distance or level, the blind man could see or discern every man clearly. He regained 20/20 vision.

When we say that we want to exchange the gift of our spouse or we lack the consideration to butter our spouse's toast, we need a vision alignment. Something has clouded our vision, and we are only seeing the negatives. Unhealthy or uncommunicated expectations may be hindering our vision. What the world views as the 80/20 rule is affecting our sight. Grudges, offenses, or unforgiveness are little foxes that spoil the vine and form spiritual scales on our eyes.

It is time for you to move away from the crowd. Distance yourself from your expectations and take your spouse to Jesus. Ask Him to align your vision so that you can see the different levels of your gift.

Now it is time to learn the healthy, divine patterns that comprise your expectations as a husband and wife. Let's process your thoughts through writing first. Paper is provided for you.

1. What life applications can you take from the verses?

2. How do you see your spouse? What expectations has he or she met? What expectations have been unmet? Have you communicated them to your spouse? Have you discussed how you felt?

3. Each distance that the blind man moved resulted in clearer sight and advanced him from level to level. As you work through the exercises, you expect your marriage to go to another level. What are your expectations for your marriage after you complete this workbook? What are your expectations for this workbook?

4. As husbands and wives, you should have 20/20 vision when it comes to your self-care and future care. Self-care and future care are a part of your gift to your spouse. Just like you would take care of your gift that someone gives you so that you can enjoy it as long as possible, you take care of yourself and your future so that your spouse and children can enjoy long life and a secure future. You need to seek some quiet time to rejuvenate and reconnect to God so that you can emotionally and spiritually prosper. You must also be physically and financially healthy so that you can live the long-life God has promised you and leave an inheritance and continued security for your families if something should happen. Assess your vision and expectations in these areas. What areas need an alignment?

5. Write a prayer asking God to help you see the gift of your spouse through His eyes. Ask Him how you can partner with Him to help accomplish the plans that He has for your spouse (Jeremiah 29:11).

My Reflections

_____

_____

_____

_____

_____

_____

_____

_____

_____

_____

_____

_____

Exercise #8
What I Like About You

Directions: This exercise is designed to help you re-envision the gift of your spouse and discover the different layers of this gift. You won't find every layer; that's what the lifetime of your marriage is for. As you grow older, the layers will adapt as a part of your personal and spiritual development. This exercise will help you appreciate your gift and see its value through God's eyes. Take a few moments to think about what you admire about your spouse and write it down.

What I Admire About My Husband

1.	
2.	
3.	
4.	
5.	

What I Admire About My Wife

1.	
2.	
3.	
4.	
5.	

Now here is the challenge. Get five bags or boxes of different sizes. You want each box or bag to fit inside each other so that it is a gift inside of a gift. Think about the five things that you admire about your spouse. Purchase or make a gift that captures each one of those things and place it inside each bag or box. The largest box or bag will be for the one thing that you admire the most. Since the bags or boxes are fitting inside of each other, the idea is to show the different layers of the gift of your spouse. Your gifts demonstrate your appreciation of your spouse. Be as creative and thoughtful as possible!

Exercise #9
Are We Meeting God's Expectations?

Read the following list of expectations. For each expectation, list examples that can be found in your marriage and list suggestions for how you can improve in each expectation.

10 Biblical Expectations of Marriage
(Not in Order)

1) Expected to honor covenant (Malachi 2:16)

_____

_____

_____

2) Expected to make each other better (Proverbs 31:23, Ephesians 5:26)

_____

_____

_____

3) Expected to meet each other's needs emotionally and sexually (I Cor. 7:3)

_____

_____

_____

4) Expected to protect from potential threats (I Samuel 30:18)

_____

_____

_____

5) Expected to pray together and for each other (Matthew 18:19)

_____

_____

_____

6) Expected to invest time in the relationship (Song of Solomon 2:10)

_____

_____

_____

7) Expected to be #2 priority in each other's lives and God to be the #1 priority (Matthew 22:37-39)

_____

_____

_____

8) Expected to leave an inheritance (Proverbs 13:22)

_____

_____

_____

9) Expected to share in decisions (Proverbs 11:14)

_____

_____

_____

10) Expected to do life together (Ecclesiastes 4:9)

_____

_____

_____

Exercise #10
What Do You Expect?

This questionnaire helps you to know your own expectations, wants, and values in your marriage. It will also help you to better understand your spouse's expectations. Fill out your answers separately, and then share your answers with each other. Your goal is to simply understand and listen to each other. Be as honest and practical as possible in your answers.

1. List 10 expectations that you have for your spouse.

Column A My Expectations for My Spouse	Column B My Spouse's Expectations for Me
1.	1.
2.	2.
3.	3.
4.	4.
5.	5.
6.	6.
7.	7.
8.	8.
9	9.
10.	10.

2. In Column A, circle 3 expectations that are most important to you.
3. In Column A, circle 3 expectations that you may need to modify or even let go.
4. Write an R next to your expectations that you believe are Reasonable.
5. Write a U next to those which could be Unreasonable.
6. Write down your partner's answers in column B in order to understand and compare with yours.
7. Discuss how to make practical adjustments to meet each other's expectations for each topic.

Exercise #11
Putting Concept into Action

1. **Destructive Patterns/Thoughts:** Criticism is at the center of the destructive pattern: I want to exchange my gift. We tend to always talk about what's not working or what our spouses are not doing right. Criticism is like a trail of ants marching through our picnics and taking away our food, piece by piece. In our marriages, those critical words and thoughts are taking away your tightknit bond, and they are pushing you further apart. When you lack consideration of your spouse by not making him or her a priority, forgetting to apologize, or not including him or her into your decisions, you do not show honor or respect.

   Lastly, what about self-care and future care? Both husband and wife should take care of their bodies and health. As the priest of the home, the husband should have all financial affairs and important documents in order to prepare for an unexpected event. What kind of inheritance will both of you leave for your children and your children's children? Think about these patterns. Make a list of 5 things you have done that fit into one of the patterns or you feel like you need to change.

   A._____

   B._____

   C._____

   D._____

   E._____

2. **Divine Patterns/Thoughts:** What would be the Biblical response to those 5 things that you have listed? How can you respond in a healthy way?

   A._____

   _____

   _____

   B._____

   _____

   _____

   C._____

   _____

   _____

D._____

_____

_____

E._____

_____

_____

3. **Developing Strategies:** Think of 3 actions that you can do to incorporate healthy, divine patterns into your relationship regarding this concern.

A._____

    1._____

    2._____

    3._____

B._____

    1._____

    2._____

    3._____

C._____

    1._____

    2._____

    3._____

D._____

    1._____

    2._____

    3._____

E._____

    1._____

    2._____

    3._____

Chapter 2 Writing Reflection
Flipping the Script on Marital Expectations

Take this time to reflect on your responses to the exercises. Go back to Exercise #1. Rank the expectations that you have for your marriage again. For the writing reflection, you are going to do something different. You have been reflecting on your expectations for your spouse and marriage. Now you are going to flip the script. What expectations do you have for yourself as a husband or a wife? How can you extend grace to yourself when you don't meet your spouse's expectations? What does God expect from you as a wife or husband? Now write your reflections below.

Wife's Reflections

_____

_____

_____

_____

_____

_____

_____

_____

_____

_____

_____

_____

_____

Husband's Reflections

_____

_____

_____

_____

_____

_____

_____

_____

_____

_____

_____

_____

_____

_____

_____

_____

_____

_____

Chapter 3

Our Open Communication

Communication is a complex dance between husband and wife. One partner must become in sync with the other partner's movements. He must read her movements, facial expressions, and anticipate in which direction she is moving. If he loses the rhythm, the choreography is off, and they look like they are not connected.

With communication, we as husbands and wives must realize that our gender differences affect how we communicate and what we expect as responses or engagement in our communication. Family background and childhood baggage also play a part in our communication. When we don't deal with those situations that we have buried underneath, they form roots in our mindsets and our hearts. Out of the abundance of our hearts, our mouths speak words that cause division in our marriages. Our communication should bring us on one accord and help us to move forward in the purpose for our marriage.

We must realize that communication styles in our families may have been different. What we are accustomed to as dialogue may offend or hurt our spouse because it varies differently from his or her household. Remember we have become one flesh. One flesh means a common style of communication that merges or adapts what was familiar in their families to one that fits our marital covenant.

Miscommunication and non-communication are at the heart of the distance that couples feel in their marriages. Loneliness and isolation settle in when the husband and wife are talking to each other, but it feels like they are not listening or understanding what they are saying or feeling. It is like the spouse has a voice, but he or she is behind the glass of soundproof room that mutes his or her words. When we do not find a common ground in our communication, our words are aiming at our ears, but they keep missing the target. Not being heard or understood is an unsettling place to be. Thoughts of why we are even here enter our minds, and the closeness starts to fade away. Communication is one of the key pillars in the foundations of our marriages.

Abram and Sarai probably experienced communication problems, among other things, in their marriage. Even though Sarai proposed the arrangement between Abram and Hagar, she didn't foresee the tension it would later cause. When Sarai complained to Abram about Hagar mocking her with contempt because of her pregnancy, Abram, like most males, didn't want to come between two women. If it is better for one to live in a corner of a housetop than dwell with a contentious woman, where can a man between two women go? He took the passive route and committed Sarai's maidservant to her hands. Sarai took her frustration out on Hagar and treated her harshly until she ran away.

We wonder if Abram and Sarai really talked this decision through. Instead of being a beacon of wisdom through prayer in her husband's decisions, ministry/spiritual development, and other marital affairs, Sarai made an unwise decision to bring another woman into her marriage to fulfill a need that God promised to do. What unhealthy patterns in communication can we find in other Biblical marriages and our own? Let's go through the following exercises and move forward toward more open communication.

Chapter 3 Objectives

- Gain revelation and understanding about your current view of communication
- Understand what can hinder your communication
- Learn about healthy patterns and perspectives regarding your communication as husband and wife
- Encourage open dialogue and improve communication between you and your spouse
- Create a deeper intimacy in your relationship as you discuss how you want your communication to change for the better
- Commit to grow in learning more about your marriage's communication styles

Negative Patterns Addressed in This Chapter

- From *Stop the Foolishness for Husbands*
  - No Words Left: Communication Woes

- From *Stop the Foolishness for Wives*
  - The Nagger
  - Where's the Wife?
  - Childhood Baggage

Exercise #1
Assessing What We Think About Our Communication

1. How would you describe the way you communicate with each other?

    _____

    _____

    _____

2. What are 3 problem areas that you notice in your communication?

    A _____

    B _____

    C _____

3. Describe the communication patterns in your childhood homes.

    _____

    _____

    _____

4. Is there any nagging or constant complaining in your communication? If so, what is the nagging usually about?

    _____

    _____

    _____

5. Are there any unresolved issues from your childhood or past relationships (romantic or family) that are still bothering you? What are they? How do they affect your communication?

    _____

    _____

    _____

6. Describe your communication style before you got married and when you were first married. What has changed since then? What do you think caused the change?

    _____

    _____

    _____

7. What do you want to change about the way you communicate with each other?

    A._____

    B _____

    C._____

    D._____

Exercise #2

Scenario #1: Examining Communication in David and Michal's Marriage

(2 Samuel 6:20-22 TLB)

Read the following Scriptures and answer the discussion questions below.

David returned to bless his family. But Michal came out to meet him and exclaimed in disgust, "How glorious the king of Israel looked today! He exposed himself to the girls along the street like a common pervert!"

David retorted, "I was dancing before the Lord who chose me above your father and his family and who appointed me as leader of Israel, the people of the Lord! So, I am willing to act like a fool in order to show my joy in the Lord. Yes, and I am willing to look even more foolish than this, but I will be respected by the girls of whom you spoke!"

Discussion Questions

1. Describe the communication style between David and Michal.
2. What unhealthy patterns are present in their communication?
3. What could they have done differently?
4. Do you think that Michal has any unresolved issues?
5. What can you learn from this example that you can apply to your communication?

Exercise #3

Scenario #2: Examining Communication in Hannah and Elkanah's Marriage (1 Samuel 1:3-8 TLB)

Read the following scriptures and answer the discussion questions below.

Each year Elkanah and his families journeyed to the Tabernacle at Shiloh to worship the Lord of the heavens and to sacrifice to him. (The priests on duty at that time were the two sons of Eli—Hophni and Phinehas.) On the day he presented his sacrifice, Elkanah would celebrate the happy occasion by giving presents to Peninnah and her children; but although he loved Hannah very much, he could give her only one present, for the Lord had sealed her womb; so, she had no children to give presents to. Peninnah made matters worse by taunting Hannah because of her barrenness. Every year it was the same—Peninnah scoffing and laughing at her as they went to Shiloh, making her cry so much she couldn't eat.

"What's the matter, Hannah?" Elkanah would exclaim. "Why aren't you eating? Why make such a fuss over having no children? Isn't having me better than having ten sons?"

Discussion Questions

1. Describe the communication style between Elkanah and Hannah.
2. What unhealthy patterns are present in their communication?
3. What could they have done differently?
4. Do you think that Hannah has any unresolved issues or baggage?
5. What can you learn from this example that you can apply to your communication?

Exercise #4

Scenario #3: Examining Communication between King Solomon and Queen of Sheba (1 Kings 10: 1-4, 6-9 TLB)

When the queen of Sheba heard how wonderfully the Lord had blessed Solomon with wisdom, she decided to test him with some hard questions. She arrived in Jerusalem with a long train of camels carrying spices, gold, and jewels; and she told him all her problems. Solomon answered all her questions; nothing was too difficult for him, for the Lord gave him the right answers every time. She soon realized that everything she had ever heard about his great wisdom was true.

She exclaimed to him, "Everything I heard in my own country about your wisdom and about the wonderful things going on here is all true. I didn't believe it until I came, but now I have seen it for myself! And really! The half had not been told me! Your wisdom and prosperity are far greater than anything I've ever heard of! Your people are happy, and your palace aides are content—but how could it be otherwise, for they stand here day after day listening to your wisdom! Blessed be the Lord your God who chose you and set you on the throne of Israel. How the Lord must love Israel—for he gave you to them as their king! And you give your people a just, good government!"

Discussion Questions

1. Describe the communication style between King Solomon and the queen of Sheba.
2. What healthy patterns are present in their communication? Are there any negative patterns?
3. What can you learn from this example that you can apply to your communication?

Exercise #5

Scenario #4: Examining Patterns in Communication

Read the following verses and answer the questions below.

Unhealthy Patterns in Communication	Healthy Patterns in Communication
There is one whose rash words are like sword thrusts (Proverbs 12:18a ESV)	Let no corrupting talk come out of your mouths, but only such as is good for building up, as fits the occasion, that it may give grace to those who hear. (Ephesians 4:29 ESV) A soft answer turns away wrath. (Proverbs 15:1a ESV)
A fool takes no pleasure in understanding, but only in expressing his opinion. (Proverbs 18:2 ESV)	Set a guard, O Lord, over my mouth; keep watch over the door of my lips! (Psalm 141:3 ESV)
If one gives an answer before he hears, it is his folly and shame. (Proverbs 18:13 ESV)	Know this, my beloved brothers: let every person be quick to hear, slow to speak, slow to anger; (James 1: 19 ESV)
But avoid irreverent babble, for it will lead people into more and more ungodliness. (2 Timothy 2:16 ESV)	Gracious words are like a honeycomb, sweetness to the soul and health to the body. (Proverbs 16:24 ESV)

Discussion Questions

1. What do you notice in the healthy and unhealthy patterns? What makes them healthy or unhealthy?
2. What unhealthy patterns from the books are present in their communication?
3. What can you learn from these verses that you can apply to your communication?

Exercise #6

Scenario #5: Examining Communication in 21st Century Marriages

Read the scenario below and answer the questions.

Fred* came home from a long day at work. Besides being tired, he was very discouraged because his manager overlooked him for a promotion. Marsha* had already been home for an hour. Fred's midnight snack dishes littered the kitchen sink, unwashed. Dirty laundry covered their bedroom floor and made its own nature trail into the hallway. He hadn't taken care of the washing machine repairs, and the kids had worn her last nerve with their consistent chatter and bickering. Now he had worn any other nerves that remained by coming home an hour late. As he greeted her, she said nothing. As Fred talked about his day and shared his emotions, she said nothing. When he went in for the kiss on her lips, she jutted out her elbow and turned her head sharply. When he asked to be held, Marsha let the floodgates open and nagged him. Fred went in the bathroom to escape; Marsha nagged through the closed door. Fred walked out and slumped on the couch and flipped the channel to the sports channel; Marsha competed with the volume of the television and raised her voice with more nagging. Fred made a beeline to the patio door and accidentally collided with five-year-old Bobby. He quickly apologized and hugged his son, but the incident caused Marsha to experience a flashback. Her uncle knocked her down repeatedly and physically abused her when she was a toddler. Rage bubbled up and spewed from her lips. Fred exited out the patio door, climbed in his car, and spent the night at his best friend's house.

*=fictitious names and situation

Discussion Questions

1. Describe the communication style between Fred and Marsha.
2. What unhealthy patterns are present in their communication?
3. What could they have done differently?
4. Do you think that Marsha has any unresolved issues or baggage?
5. What can you learn from this example that you can apply to your communication?

Exercise #7
Writing Prompts

In John 21:15-17, we see the art of the question. Consistent or repetitive questions can irritate, frustrate, or alienate couples. They impede conversations from being productive or progressive. When God asks us a question, He usually has a reason. He may be trying to course correct, clarify, or confirm. When Jesus talked with Peter, He had already been resurrected. Peter had been mourning, along with the other disciples, for his beloved teacher. He took it the hardest because guilt and remorse plagued him. The one who was destined to build Jesus Christ's church had cut a soldier's ear in anger and denied Christ three times. Peter had gone back to his past occupation. Jesus knew Peter would deny him because the enemy wanted to sift him like wheat. Peter was in the middle of testing and transition.

Jesus came back for Peter to give him the aid of an Advocate, the Holy Spirit, to carry out his kingdom purpose. Jesus had to clarify with Peter if he still understood what that mission was. He asked Peter the same question three times. Each time, he gave Jesus the same answer. With the third question, Peter was very hurt. Those questions served as a means of achieving clarity about what it means to function in his mission and what it really means to love Christ. As husbands and wives, our communication may be filled with more telling and complaining than asking to understand and clarify. Our questions may be a little accusatory or yes/no traps designed to prove a point. It is time to reflect on what you have discussed so far and how you and your spouse communicate with each other.

1. Think about how Jesus communicated with Peter and the other disciples. Think about how He communicated and interacted with people during His ministry. This relationship between them is more than a teacher and His disciples. It is a model of a Bridegroom with His Church. What lessons about communication can you apply to your marital communication style?

2. What kind of love was Christ talking about in His questions? What kind of love was Peter talking about in his responses? How can you reflect love in your verbal and nonverbal communication? Have your past conversations during the past week reflected love?

3. Come up with ten questions to ask your spouse. The purpose of the questions is to seek to understand, to clarify, or to draw closer. Ask them in an intimate setting. Reflect on your conversation.

Reflections

Exercise #8
Cleaning Our Filters

Social media sites such as Facebook and Instagram have popularized the filter. It can change our photos and other images to whatever we want it to be. Each of us have a filter. It is a way we receive information from conversations or any other interactions that we have. Filters separate out what they want to keep and what they want to release. For example, water filters separate sediments and other particles from the water so that the drinking water is purified. The water entered the filter one way, but it came out another way. It has been changed for the better.

Filters are gates. Our marriages, our minds, our mouths, and our hearts have gates that allow access. What we receive can have a positive or negative effect on us mentally, emotionally, and spiritually. We must guard our gates, assess the state of what the gates guard, and adjust our filters. Our communication flows from words that come out of our mouths. Remember our mouths are one of those major gates.

Think about your conversations throughout your marriage. What words, conversations, or experiences have had a negative effect? What words, conversations, or experiences have had a positive effect? What have your conversations allowed to enter your minds, hearts, and marriage? What needs to be filtered out of your communication? What needs to be maintained or kept in your communication? What unhealthy patterns do you notice?

Directions: For the following exercise on the next page, you will see two boxes with an arrow between them. In the first box, write down your responses to the questions listed above. In the arrow, write down what you want to remove out of your communication (what needs to be filtered out for your communication to become more open and healthier). In the second box, write down what you want to remain in your communication. Once the unhealthy and negative things have been filtered out, what will your communication look like now?

WHAT OUR COMMUNICATION HAS NOW
(Responses to the questions in the exercise)

FILTER

WHAT OUR COMMUNICATION LOOKS LIKE NOW
(Responses to the questions in the exercise)

Exercise #9
Putting Concept into Action

1. **Destructive Patterns/Thoughts:** We have learned that gender differences, nagging, and baggage from childhood and past relationships/experiences affect our communication and interaction with each other. As a husband and wife, we must have each other backs. Not only does the wife have to provide wise and gentle counsel to her husband in his ministry, decisions/judgments, basic grooming/self-care, maintenance of sexual purity, and prayer, but the husband should do the same for his wife. Both of you are a team, a partnership, a cohesive unit---that one flesh! So your team needs to function better on this mission field of ministering to others through your marriage. Identify areas that needs to be addressed. Think about the patterns from the chapters in our books. Make a list of five (5) things you have done that fit into one of the patterns or you feel like you need to change.

    A._____

    B._____

    C._____

    D._____

    E._____

2. **Divine Patterns/Thoughts:** What would be the Biblical response to those five (5) things that you have listed? How can you communicate in a healthy way?

    A._____

    B._____

    C._____

    D._____

    E._____

3. **Developing Strategies:** Think of three (3) actions that you can do to incorporate healthy, divine patterns into your relationship regarding this concern.

    A._____

      1._____

      2._____

      3._____

STOP THE FOOLISHNESS FOR COUPLES

B._____

    1._____

    2._____

    3._____

C._____

    1._____

    2._____

    3._____

D._____

    1._____

    2._____

    3._____

E._____

    1._____

    2._____

    3._____

Chapter 3 Writing Reflection & Hands-On Activity
Creating a Vision Board for Our Communication

Take this time to reflect on your responses to the exercises. Vision boards are often used to cut out pictures and words that illustrate a goal that we want to achieve. Your goal is your communication. You have worked through the exercises and hopefully have discovered some healthy patterns you want to implement into your communication. Remember the goal is have communication that is open and healthy. If you were to create a vision board, write down the things you would include on it. Describe how it would look. Once you write your thoughts down as a couple, get a poster board, trifold, or find an app and create the vision board. Before you start this exercise, pray with your spouse. Allow the Lord to be the author of your vision and faith. Now write your reflections below.

Our Reflections

_____

_____

_____

_____

_____

_____

_____

_____

_____

_____

_____

Chapter 4

Our Prayer Life

Another key part of our communication is a devotional life centered around God. We as husbands and wives need to have our own personal time to engage with God in prayer, meditation, reading the Bible, and worship. Once we meet with Him personally, then we meet corporately as a couple. The anchor of our devotional lives is prayer. It is a two-way communication that grounds us in our relationship with God and determines the direction of our day.

When a ship is docked at the port, the captain lowers the anchor to secure its position. Storms may come with rocky waves and turbulent winds. The ship will sway a little, but the anchor keeps it firmly rooted to the ground. Our marriages will undergo the storms of life from time to time. A devotional life full of fervent prayer will help us remain steadfast and immoveable as we abound in love and excellence in our marriages to the glory of God.

Not only does prayer keep us steady during difficult times, but it also helps us remain stable in our emotions and thoughts throughout our day. Jesus is the perfect model of a person relying on prayer. Early in the morning or after a long time of ministry, He always separated Himself from people and withdrew to a quiet place to pray.

Morning time prayer strengthened Jesus for the day. He constantly had performed miracles, taught in the synagogue, ministered to people, and trained his emerging apostolic team of disciples. Prayer gave Him wisdom and direction to accomplish these tasks. Jesus also faced opposition from the Pharisees. They often formed crowds to kill him, but Jesus knew His purpose was to die on the cross to save mankind. The intimate conversation with His Father in prayer reminded Him of His purpose and prevented Him from reacting to opposition in His flesh.

We as husbands have a purpose in our marriage to take responsibility, cultivate, provide security and stability in our homes, serve as a priest, and take control over our spiritual atmosphere. We as wives have a purpose to be a helper. We are the spiritual generals that partner with our husbands in prayer. Husbands and wives work together to fulfill the Genesis mandate of being fruitful, multiplying, filling the earth, subduing it, and having dominion.

Our daily lives can be hectic. As soon as the alarm clock buzzes, our minds may race with thoughts of what to do, where to go, and where we will get the energy to do everything. We must be careful. Busyness is a distraction. It gets our minds off praying, and we neglect our posts in our marriages and homes. Vulnerable points are left open for spiritual attacks.

Prayer is essential for us as couples. We witness in the first book of the Bible that the devil's first attack on earth was through the family. He began with the marriage by causing dissension and confusion that led to separation from God, hard labor for Adam, and removal from the Garden of Eden. That vulnerable point widened to a breach that led to one son being murdered and another being marked as a vagabond. Learn how to become effective in prayer and intercession so that you can guard your marriage, family, home, purpose, and future. This chapter will be different.

Chapter 4 Objectives

- Gain revelation and understanding about your current view of prayer
- Learn about healthy patterns and perspectives regarding your prayer life
- Encourage open dialogue and improve communication between you and your spouse
- Create a deeper intimacy in your relationship as you discuss how you want your prayer life to change for the better
- Commit to grow in learning more about your prayer life

Negative Patterns Addressed in This Chapter

- From *Stop the Foolishness for Husbands*
    - The King Has Left the Building
    - Doing Marriage in the Lord

- From *Stop the Foolishness for Wives*
    - Too Weak to Fight
    - The Journey Continues

Exercise #1
Begin with Prayer

Before you complete this assessment, let's begin with engaging in the topic at hand. Let's begin with prayer. There is an acronym often used as a model for prayer: ACTS. *A* stands for adoration unto God, *C* stands for confession in which we take our sins to God and repent, *T* is for thanksgiving in which we express gratitude to God for all He has done, and then last is *S* for supplication in which we make our requests known unto Him. We are going to adapt this model to seek the Lord in prayer before we complete the chapter exercises. Find a quiet place in your home for you and your husband to write the prayer together and then pray it aloud. Here is the model:

A   Love on God with adoration. Declare who He is and who He has been in your marriage.

C   Confess your faults and sins to the Lord. Ask for forgiveness and repent.

T   Thank God for who He is and what He has done. Thank Him for covering your marriage.

S   Make your requests know for marital concerns. Take turns interceding for each other. Ask God what he wants you learn from this chapter and how He wants you to improve your prayer life.

Our Prayer

_____

_____

_____

_____

_____

_____

_____

_____

_____

_____

_____

_____

Exercise #2
Our Current Marital Status
(Assessing where we are in our marriage and prayer life)

Now it is time for you to assess where you are in your marriage and prayer life. Answer the following questions.

1. Where are you right now? Where are you physically, spiritually, mentally, emotionally, and relationally?

_____

_____

_____

2. What is the current state of your marriage?

_____

_____

_____

3. How would you describe your prayer life right now? When do you pray? Do you have a certain time that you pray together and individually? Do you write your prayers in a journal or notebook and date them when God answers them? How do you pray for each other and your marriage?

_____

_____

_____

4. What are the strengths of your marriage?

_____

_____

_____

5. What are your husband's strengths?

_____

_____

_____

6. What are your wife's strengths?

_____

_____

_____

7. What are some areas in your marriage that you need to improve?

_____

_____

_____

8. What are some things that are negatively impacting your marriage?

_____

_____

_____

9. What are some things that may be a threat to your unity?

_____

_____

_____

10. What opportunities for growth do you see for your marriage?

_____

_____

_____

_____

11. What is the current state of your relationship with God?

_____

_____

_____

12. Describe your devotional life.

_____

_____

_____

13. What opportunities for growth do you see for your relationship with God?

_____

_____

_____

_____

14. Now write a prayer to God about your current marital status.

_____

_____

_____

_____

_____

_____

Exercise #3
Checking the Fruit of Our Mandate

Answer the following questions.

A. Purpose

1. As a husband or wife, what do you perceive your purpose to be (relationally and personally)?
2. Do you feel like you are doing well in your purpose? What do you feel like you need to improve?
3. What kind of fruit have you produced in your purpose?
4. How does your husband or wife support you in your purpose? What do you need from her or him to help you?

B. Be Fruitful

5. Discuss where you have the fruit of love in your marriage.
6. Discuss where you have the fruit of joy in your marriage.
7. Discuss where you have the fruit of peace in your marriage.
8. Discuss where you have the fruit of patience in your marriage.
9. Discuss where you have the fruit of kindness in your marriage.
10. Discuss where you have the fruit of goodness in your marriage.
11. Discuss where you have the fruit of faithfulness in your marriage.
12. Discuss where you have the fruit of gentleness in your marriage.
13. Discuss where you have the fruit of self-control in your marriage.
14. Which of the fruit are not present in your marriage? How can you produce it? What needs to change or improve?

C. Multiply and Fill in the Earth

15. What seeds have you planted in your marriage that have multiplied in positive ways?
16. How are you as a couple influencing those around you with your marriage?
17. What impact or influence are you having in the world through your individual purpose?
18. How can you make more impact, multiply your witness, and fill in the earth with your influence as husband and wife?

19. What younger married couples or engaged couples can you mentor? What lessons have you learned that you can pour into them as a part of your mandate to multiply and fill in the earth?

D. Subdue and Have Dominion

20. What has tried to subdue your mind, heart, spirit, or marriage?
21. How did you handle it? Did you have a prayer strategy?
22. What area of your life do you have dominion? What does that look like? Do you think of dominion as control or authority? How does one exercise his or her authority in a godly way?

Now reflect on your answers. Decide on three to five prayer points and write a prayer.

Our Prayer

_____

_____

_____

_____

_____

_____

_____

_____

_____

_____

_____

_____

Exercise #4
Prayer Targets

For this exercise, you are going to review the exercises from the four chapters that you have completed, pick three prayer targets, find Scriptures for your prayer targets, and write your prayer including all three prayer targets and the words from your Scriptures. Once you write a prayer, set a certain time to meditate, worship, and then pray your prayer. Decide as a couple or follow the Lord's leading on how long to pray this prayer. Whatever you decide, consistency, expectation, and faith are important.

Prayer Targets

A._____

B._____

C._____

Bible Verses

Prayer Target #1	**Prayer Target #2**	**Prayer Target #3**
1._____	1._____	1._____
2._____	2._____	2._____
3._____	3._____	3._____

Our Prayer

_____

_____

_____

_____

_____

_____

Chapter 4 Writing Reflection
Creating Our Marital Mission Statement & Vision

Take this time to reflect on your responses to the exercises. Every organization has a brand identity. It is the image that the organization wants to be known for in the its industry. The organization creates a mission statement that identifies who it is, what they strive to do, and how it wants to influence its territory. The mission statement is often followed by a vision. The vision describes where the company wants to be after it accomplishes its mission. You are going to write a mission statement and vision for your marriage. Before you start, review the opening exercise of this workbook.

Step 1:   Generate a list of twenty words or phrases that describe what you want your marriage to be.

Step 2:   Write three things that you want to strive to do and three ways you want to influence your territory.

Step 3:   Write your thoughts about where you want your marriage to be in five years.

Step 4:   Write your marital mission statement in 75 words.

Step 5:   Write your marital vision statement in 35 words.

Step 6:   Write three core principles to develop in your marriage.

Step 7:   Develop an action plan on how to accomplish your mission and vision. Include dates to review your progress quarterly.

Step 8:   Lay what you have written before the Lord in prayer. Pray over it daily.

Our Marital Mission Statement and Vision

_____

_____

_____

_____

_____

_____

_____

PART 2

OBJECTIVES

The purpose of Part 2 is two-fold: 1) to help you further unpack the concepts discussed in *Stop the Foolishness for Husbands* and *Stop the Foolishness for Wives* and 2) to find common ground in your finances, family life, and intimacy. We want you to go deeper into self-examination so you can become the best version of yourselves for your marriage. As a couple, you will evaluate and assess where you are individually and relationally in your marriages by completing exercises that cover the following objectives:

- Find common ground in your marriage
- Devise strategies for your finances
- Discuss and evaluate your parenting style
- Assess relationships between you and your in-laws
- Improve your family life and intimacy
- Maintain the health of your marriage
- Identify and eliminate small, destructive patterns
- Foster intimacy and patience
- Understand different needs and perspectives for each other
- Honor each other
- Rebuild and repair relationships
- Reignite passion (especially for those who have been married a long time)
- Take responsibility for the positive and negative contributions to the relationship
- Identify and implement healthy patterns
- Devise action steps and develop strategies to strengthen your marriage
- Create a mission statement and vision for your finances
- Create a family life contract
- Write goals, affirmations, and a prayer for your marriage
- Write love letters to each other

DIAGNOSTIC ASSESSMENT

Directions: After reading the passage, write your answers to the following questions.

In geometry, there are often two lines that are not connected, but they are going in the same direction. The lines soon find a point of convergence where they meet to form an angle. The angle may be as wide as a line or as small as an acute angle. The lines may be of different sizes or shapes, but they still find a point of convergence. How far they open indicates their reach or a boundary that marks their territory. The lines have put aside trying to go in their own direction and find a common point to agree.

We as couples must find common ground. We may differ in opinions or experience conflicts, but we must iron out our differences and walk in agreement. If Jesus came to the earth to remove the dividing wall between Jews and Gentiles to unify them, then He intends for husbands and wives to have no walls between them. He came to remove anything blocking us from having a common ground in Him through salvation. Jesus honored covenant. We must honor covenant as well.

This chapter covers topics that can cause division in our marriages. Before we start, it is imperative that you and your spouse are honest and transparent with each other. You cannot fix what you will not face. It is a trendy quote, but there is a truth in it. Let's move forward to stop the foolishness in our marriages and find common ground.

1. What areas of your marriage have you established a common ground?

   _____

   _____

   _____

2. What areas of your marriage do you need to find a common ground?

   _____

   _____

   _____

3. Where have lines or boundaries been crossed in your marriage? Which ones need to be redefined?

_____

_____

_____

4. What offenses do you have toward your spouse?

_____

_____

_____

_____

5. Describe the current state of your finances and your intimacy.

_____

_____

_____

_____

6. Describe the current state of your sex life.

_____

_____

_____

_____

7. Describe the current state of your relationship with your in-laws. How do you handle conflicts with them and with each other? How do you maintain peace in your marriage?

_____

_____

_____

_____

_____

8. Describe your parenting styles. How do you feel about your relationship with your children?

_____

_____

_____

9. Do you still feel like you have your identity in this marriage, or do you feel like you have lost yourself? Discuss your feelings with each other.

_____

_____

_____

_____

10. What do you want to accomplish at the end of this workbook?

_____

_____

_____

_____

Chapter 5

Our Finances

To whom much is given, much is required. When we are faithful with a few things, we will be faithful with much. We are purposed to live a life of provision and prosperity, but we must be disciplined, wise, and diligent in how we handle it. Finances can be a thing of happiness or a source of contention in our marriages based on how we value and manage them.

Good financial management begins with position. We must realize that God is the Source. He has commissioned us to be stewards or managers of His resources that He has entrusted to us. He is first, not mortgage or rent, daycare expenses, car notes, or student loans. Money is not in control. It is a servant. If we seek the kingdom of God and His righteousness, all these things will be added unto us. We must invite Jesus to take His place in our finances.

We must put things in order—our thoughts and values about money and finances. King Solomon stated that he saw something out of order: servants riding on horses and princes walking on the earth (Ecclesiastes 10:7 KJV). We are set apart from the world, so why are we striving to become so much like it? We are sons and daughters of the kingdom; we don't follow trends: we set them!

Debt was never meant to be our portion. When we strive to be like the world and covet material things, mismanage what we have, lose our diligence in our work ethic, or fail to prepare for the future or financial crises, then we have placed money, debt, or lack on the horses or in the positions of authority where we are supposed to be. These unhealthy patterns filter into our marriages and slowly diminish our intimacy, our connection, and our trust.

Good financial management also includes planning. The widow in 2 Kings 4 came to prophet Elisha when her husband's death left her and her sons in the hands of the debt collectors. The husband managed his ministerial affairs with excellence, but his family affairs lacked the same diligence. Jesus even told his disciples to count the cost before starting any type of vision or project. To count the cost means to use wisdom, knowledge, understanding, and financial prudence. He also shared a parable of talents that instructed the disciples to manage whatever God gives them wisely.

As husbands and wives, we must partner together to budget, plan, save, and consider each other before we spend or make any financial decision. Like the Lord told Joshua when Moses died and the responsibility of leading the people to their promised land transferred to him, we must be strong and courageous because our families and future generations are depending on us for an inheritance. We must have good work ethics and sound financial judgment.

Good financial management includes prayer and patience. We must be prayerful about our financial decisions and practice patience when pursuing financial goals and vision. It takes time to build our financial future and wisdom to maintain it. We must fearlessly examine our habits, mindsets, and childhood backgrounds to identify unhealthy patterns and roots and replace them with healthy ones through the power of the Holy Spirit. As husbands, we create the vision for our finances and entrust our wives to build it with us. We both must do our part. Let's get to work!

Chapter 5 Objectives

- Gain revelation and understanding about your current view of your finances
- Learn about healthy patterns and perspectives regarding your finances
- Encourage open dialogue and improve communication between you and your spouse
- Create a deeper intimacy in your relationship as you discuss how you want your finances to change for the better
- Commit to grow in learning about how to maintain a healthy financial lifestyle

Negative Patterns Addressed in This Chapter

- From *Stop the Foolishness for Husbands*
  - No Romance Without Finance

- From *Stop the Foolishness for Wives*
  - What about the Joneses?

Exercise #1_____
Assessing What We Know About Our Finances

Answer the following questions.

1. How did your parents handle finances? What do you remember about your family's financial health while you were growing up?

_____

_____

_____

_____

_____

2. How is your faith married to your finances?

_____

_____

_____

_____

3. Who handles the finances in your marriage? Why? If you are not handling the finances, how do you support your spouse?

_____

_____

_____

_____

4. What are three positive things that you can say about your finances?
   A. _____
   B. _____
   C. _____

5. What are three things that you are dissatisfied with or need to improve about your finances?
   A._____
   B._____
   C._____

6. If you could create your ideal financial outlook, what would it be?

7. What system(s) do you have in place for managing money?

8. What financial goals have you set? How often do you set them: monthly, quarterly, or annually?

9. What do you have in place to handle emergencies or crises?

10. How is your savings? How can you improve your savings or bring in different streams of income?

11. What plans do you have in place for retirement?

_____
_____
_____
_____
_____

12. What plans do you have in place if something were to happen to one of you?

_____
_____
_____
_____
_____

13. What is your personal work ethic? How does it affect your family's financial health?

Husband: _____

_____
_____
_____
_____

Wife: _____

_____
_____
_____
_____

Exercise #2

Scenario #1: The Basics of Kingdom Finances

Read the following verses and answer the following questions.

- And my God will supply every need of yours according to his riches in glory in Christ Jesus. (Philippians 4:19 ESV)
- Keep your life free from love of money, and be content with what you have, for he has said, "I will never leave you nor forsake you." (Hebrews 13:5 ESV)
- The blessing of the Lord makes rich, and he adds no sorrow with it. (Proverbs 10:22 ESV)
- Honor the Lord with your wealth and with the firstfruits of all your produce; then your barns will be filled with plenty, and your vats will be bursting with wine. (Proverbs 3:9-10 ESV)
- And God is able to make all grace abound to you, so that having all sufficiency in all things at all times, you may abound in every good work. (2 Corinthians 9:8 ESV)

Discussion Questions

1. How would you define provision? How has God provided for you?
2. What is your idea of being financially blessed?
3. What does it mean to be content? Are you content right now?
4. What do you need God to supply in your finances?
5. What does it look like to be financially stable according to kingdom standards?

Exercise #3

Scenario #2: The Principle of Diligence

- The plans of the diligent lead surely to abundance, but everyone who is hasty comes only to poverty. (Proverbs 21:5 ESV)

- The hand of the diligent will rule, while the slothful will be put to forced labor. (Proverbs 12:24 ESV)

- Love not sleep, lest you come to poverty; open your eyes, and you will have plenty of bread. (Proverbs 20:13 ESV)

- The soul of the sluggard craves and gets nothing, while the soul of the diligent is richly supplied. (Proverbs 13:4 ESV)

- Seest thou a man diligent in his business? he shall stand before kings; he shall not stand before mean men. (Proverbs 22:29 KJV)

- And let us not grow weary of doing good, for in due season we will reap, if we do not give up. (Galatians 6:9 ESV)

Discussion Questions

1. Discuss what diligence means to you.
2. How have you been diligent in your marriage, employment, and finances?
3. Where have you experienced weariness in your finances?
4. Do you have any practices in place that may lead to poverty?
5. How do you honor God in your finances?

Exercise #4

Scenario #3: Examining Finances in 21st Century Marriages

Rick* and Linda Jo* lived in a beautiful, two-story house in an upper class, gated subdivision. They both owned matching Jaguar coupes, hers was red and his black. Rick was an executive at Merrill Lynch, and his wife was a tenured professor at the local university. Both of their salaries combined equaled six figures. Overdue bills littered their dining room table. They never kept a budget or managed money efficiently. They were all for living in the moment. Linda Jo had to have the latest Brahmin bags and designer clothes. Rick loved high quality golf clubs and expensive watches. Neither of them tithed. They gave generous offerings, usually when there was a need or a call to give for a cause.

Something unexpected happened. Doctors diagnosed Rick with stage 4 prostate cancer. His health deteriorated quickly. During this time, Linda Jo's university had budget cuts, and her classes were given to adjuncts. Medical bills depleted a lot of their finances, and they had no savings or crisis management plan. Now one of their Jags has been repossessed, and they are in danger of foreclosure. Depression and despair had filled their hearts and impacted their marriage. Rick and Linda Jo were hanging on by a thread.

*=fictitious names and situation

Discussion Questions:

1. How would you describe this couple's financial status?
2. What unhealthy patterns do you see in their marriage?
3. What could they have done differently?
4. What position did money have in their lives?

Exercise #5
Writing Prompt

A philosophy is a guiding set of beliefs that govern the way a person thinks or acts. For example, teachers often have a philosophy regarding their methodologies and views of student learning. Doctors may give their philosophy on their medical practices. Our finances are governed by our philosophy, the way we think about money, and how it should be managed. We must challenge what isn't working, create a vision for our finances, and implement changes to improve our finances.

You are going to write your financial philosophy for this exercise. Below are the items you will include in it. Paper is provided for you.

Our Financial Philosophy

- Our Beliefs about Finances
- Our Values about Finances
- My Role as a Husband in Our Finances
- My Role as a Wife in Our Finances
- Beliefs We Want to Instill in Our Children
- Our System for Managing Expenses
- Our System for Savings & Future Planning
- Our Mission Statement for Our Finances
- Our Vision for Our Finances
- Our Financial Goals

Our Financial Philosophy

Exercise #6
Putting Concept into Action

Now it is time to put the concept into action. Review your responses to the assessments and exercises for this chapter. Reflect on what you have read in our books. You are going to think about five actions or situations regarding your roles that you want to improve. These actions deal with the destructive, unhealthy patterns that we have written about regarding roles. Once you list those patterns, actions, or situations, you are going to write a Biblical response to them that would involve a healthy, divine pattern. Then you will create action steps to help you implement the healthy patterns. This exercise will be in most of the chapters. You can return to the following example for future exercises.

Example from Discussion Scenario #4:

Destructive Pattern/Thought: My husband and I do not keep track of our finances. We love to live in the moment. I love buying Brahmin handbags and driving my Jag because it is a status symbol. Everyone who is a person of influence in my city have expensive possessions.

Divine Pattern/Thought: In the parable of the talents, the person in charge gave each servant a set amount to manage until he returned. King Solomon says in Ecclesiastes that it is a gift of God to work and have daily provision. My husband and I should work unto the glory of God. We must gain approval from Him and only be concerned with what He thinks. I need to let go of the approval of men and comparing myself to others. My husband is sick, and we are struggling. Change has to begin with me in better management of our finances.

Developing Strategies: Step one is for me to gather all our bills and record it in a notebook. I need to contact each company and make payment arrangements. I will apply to other local colleges for part-time or full-time teaching positions. I may even try going into the public-school system. I need to create a monthly budget and record all expenses. Since I have no experience in managing money, I probably need to seek a financial planner or counselor as a mentor and accountability partner.

Your Turn:

1. **Destructive Patterns/Thoughts:** Unhealthy patterns in our finances involve more than mismanagement. Many couples experience problems with intimacy when they are facing difficulties in their finances. Physical touch decreases, sex is withheld as punishment, or communication is more about finances and complaints instead of loving and encouraging each other. Unhealthy patterns in our finances deal with our identities. If one of us has been out of work for a long time or if a financial crisis overstays its welcome, it can affect how we feel about ourselves.

   Low self-esteem, depression, oppression, resentment, manipulation, control, and hopelessness are some of the emotional and spiritual strongholds that can cause problems with our intimacy and our marriage. Again, it is all about order. Money or financial stability and status do not define us. They do not control our intimacy or our marriage. We need faith in God to supply all our needs when we keep Him first.

   Think about cycles. Are you in one now, or are you practicing unhealthy patterns that can lead to cycles? What patterns are you repeating that continue to yield the same unproductive results?

   Are you consistently arguing over finances? Be honest and transparent and write 5 things that need to be addressed.

   A. _____

   B. _____

   C. _____

   D. _____

   E. _____

2. **Divine Patterns/Thoughts:** What would be the Biblical response to those 5 things that you have listed? How can you respond in a healthy way?

   A._____

   _____

   _____

   B._____

   _____

   _____

C._____

_____

_____

D._____

_____

_____

E. _____

_____

_____

3. **Developing Strategies:** Think of 3 actions that you can do to incorporate healthy, divine patterns into your relationship regarding this concern.

    A._____

        1. _____

        2. _____

        3. _____

    B._____

        1. _____

        2. _____

        3. _____

    C. _____

        1. _____

        2. _____

        3. _____

D. _____

    1. _____
    2. _____
    3. _____

E. _____

    1. _____

    2. _____
    3. _____

Chapter 5 Writing Reflection
Creating Our Financial Plan

Take this time to reflect on your responses to the exercises. For the writing reflection, you are going to create a financial plan. Think about your monthly budget: your monthly income, your monthly bills, your financial goals, your savings, your retirement, and your future. Create a financial plan to address how you will handle your finances moving forward. In the plan, include a contract in which you decide how you will handle conflicts or disagreements about finances in a healthy way. You want to recreate your intimacy and maintain it. Brainstorm ways to bring multiple streams of income into your home. You may even have to do some downsizing such as maybe let go of that Netflix subscription or daily Starbucks run. You need to plan out how you are going to build your financial vision so that you are financially stable as a couple. Now write your reflections below.

Our Reflections

_____

_____

_____

_____

_____

_____

_____

_____

_____

_____

_____

_____

_____

_____

_____

_____

_____

_____

Chapter 6

Our Family Life

Children are a gift from the Lord. As parents, we are to train them up in the way that they should go by directing their spiritual development, nurturing their spiritual gifts, and giving them a firm foundation in who they are. Our parenting styles are influenced by the way we were raised. We find a common ground in the best way we want to raise our children.

Part of that common ground involves sharing all the responsibilities in taking care of them. One spouse shouldn't carry the whole load. If a spouse feels like he or she is doing mostly everything, then he or she may feel resentment. Our parenting styles must take into consideration the fact that both of us need to take a hands-on, physically present approach with our kids.

We must also reach a common ground on setting boundaries between our parenting time and couple time. Raising our children is a time-consuming task, but we still need to make time for each other and ourselves. When we make our children first, we lose our bond and our identity. We as husbands and wives need time to reconnect with each other and rekindle the flame of love.

Rebekah didn't maintain a common ground in parenting with her husband, Isaac (Genesis 27). They had twin boys, Jacob and Esau. Rebekah favored Jacob. Knowing that her husband couldn't see well, she told Jacob to deceive Isaac by pretending to be Esau so that he could receive the firstborn's blessing. Her actions showed that she made Jacob a priority instead of her husband. She caused a serious division in her family and her marriage. As parents, we shouldn't make our children our best thing. We have a marriage covenant with each other, not our children.

We also must remember that our marriage covenant excludes our in-laws. When we become one flesh, we stop running to our parents with our problems. Their input in our marital and family affairs ends at the altar when "I do" seals the covenant. We do not forsake their sage wisdom, but there shouldn't be a competition or comparison between them and your spouse. We do not disconnect from our families; we are a unit, but our marital covenants are between husband and wife.

Boundaries must be gracefully and tactfully established and maintained through love and peace with our children and in-laws. A great, and probably least thought of example is Mary, mother of Jesus. Jesus spent three years in His ministry, and His ministry was reconciling His bride to the One who had sent Him.

In Mark 3:31-35 KJV, His mother, Mary, and Jesus' brothers came to where He was teaching one day. They sent someone to call him. Then the multitude told him what was going on. Jesus responded, "Who is my mother, or my brethren?" He proclaimed they were his mother and brothers, if they do the will of God. Mary didn't get offended and claim mother immunity. She didn't force her way in to see him. She respected His relationship with His bride.

Let's go through the following exercises and move forward to healthier patterns in our relationships with our parents, children, and each other.

Chapter 6 Objectives

- Gain revelation and understanding about your current view of your parenting style and family life
- Learn about healthy patterns and perspectives regarding your relationships with your children and in-laws
- Encourage open dialogue and improve communication about your children and in-laws between you and your spouse
- Create a deeper intimacy in your relationship as you discuss how you want your family life to change for the better
- Commit to grow in learning more about how to achieve a healthy balance between your marriage and your family life

Negative Patterns Addressed in This Chapter

- From *Stop the Foolishness for Husbands*
  - Your Children First
  - Apron Strings: Your Wife Is Not Your Mother

- From *Stop the Foolishness for Wives*
  - What about the Children?
  - In-Law Interference

Exercise #1
Assessing What We Think About Our Family Life

These exercises are opportunities for you to be honest and transparent with each other. Parenting and in-laws can be sensitive subjects for husbands and wives. This is not an open door for attacks, negative words, or any other unhealthy communication. You are trying to be open in sharing what you feel, listen with empathetic hearts, ask God for the right way to respond, seek a way to acknowledge each other's feelings, and find a divine and practical solution. You want to draw nigh to the Lord and to each other, and not find yourselves further apart.

Answer the following questions.

1. What do you want to improve about your family life?

_____

_____

_____

_____

2. Describe your spouse's relationship with your parents.

_____

_____

_____

_____

3. What do you want to improve about your spouse's relationship with your parents?

_____

_____

_____

_____

4. Name three things that you love about each of your children. What makes each one unique?

_____

_____

_____

_____

5. Have you asked God what His purpose is for each of your children? Have you asked Him how you can partner with Him to aid in the spiritual development of your children? If you do know the purpose for each of your children, what have you done to help nurture each one in it?

_____

_____

_____

_____

6. Do you have family meetings, prayer time, or devotional time? How do you grow closer as a family?

_____

_____

_____

_____

7. What concerns you the most about your parenting style and your family life?

_____

_____

_____

_____

8. How would you describe your husband's relationship with his parents? Is there any aspect of it that makes you feel like you are not a priority? Discuss your concerns with your husband.

_____

_____

_____

_____

9. How would you describe your wife's relationship with her parents? Is there any aspect of it that makes you feel like you are not a priority? Discuss your concerns with your wife.

_____

_____

_____

_____

10. Have you ever felt like you were more like a parent to your spouse? If so, how does that make you feel? What do you need to change?

_____

_____

_____

_____

11. How would you describe your spouse's level of support of you when it comes to your in-laws?

_____

_____

_____

_____

12. Is there anything out of order or any confusion in your marriage when it comes to your children or in-laws? What do you need to change?

_____

_____

_____

_____

13. Think about the points of dissension or disagreement between you and your spouse. If you could make a pie chart that identifies the percentages of the root causes, what percentage would belong to your in-laws and your children? If it would help, draw a pie chart below.

_____

_____

_____

_____

Exercise #2

Scenario #1: Healthy Patterns of Biblical In-Law Relationships
(Ruth 1:6-18 NKJV)

Read the following verses and answer the questions below.

Then she arose with her daughters-in-law that she might return from the country of Moab, for she had heard in the country of Moab that the LORD had visited His people by giving them bread. Therefore, she went out from the place where she was, and her two daughters-in-law with her; and they went on the way to return to the land of Judah. And Naomi said to her two daughters-in-law, "Go, return each to her mother's house. The LORD deal kindly with you, as you have dealt with the dead and with me. The LORD grant that you may find rest, each in the house of her husband." So, she kissed them, and they lifted up their voices and wept. And they said to her, "Surely we will return with you to your people." But Naomi said, "Turn back, my daughters; why will you go with me? *Are* there still sons in my womb, that they may be your husbands? Turn back, my daughters, go—for I am too old to have a husband. If I should say I have hope, *if* I should have a husband tonight and should also bear sons, would you wait for them till they were grown? Would you restrain yourselves from having husbands? No, my daughters; for it grieves me very much for your sakes that the hand of the LORD has gone out against me!"

Then they lifted up their voices and wept again; and Orpah kissed her mother-in-law, but Ruth clung to her. And she said, "Look, your sister-in-law has gone back to her people and to her gods; return after your sister-in-law." But Ruth said: "Entreat me not to leave you, *or to* turn back from following after you; for wherever you go, I will go; and wherever you lodge, I will lodge; Your people *shall be* my people, and your God, my God. Where you die, I will die, and there will I be buried. The LORD do so to me, and more also, If *anything but* death parts you and me." When she saw that she was determined to go with her, she stopped speaking to her.

Discussion Questions

1. How would you describe the relationship between Naomi and her daughters-in-law? Do you think there were healthy patterns in their relationship when her sons were living?
2. What can you learn from this passage about how to interact with in-laws?
3. What do you think about Orpah's decision to leave?
4. If something were to happen to you, what are your expectations for your spouse regarding his or her relationship with your in-laws?

Exercise #3

Scenario #2: Unhealthy Patterns of Biblical In-Law Relationships
(Genesis 38:11-26 NKJV)

Read the following verses and answer the questions below.

Then Judah said to Tamar his daughter-in-law, "Remain a widow in your father's house till my son Shelah is grown." For he said, "Lest he also die like his brothers." And Tamar went and dwelt in her father's house. Now in the process of time the daughter of Shua, Judah's wife, died; and Judah was comforted, and went up to his sheepshearers at Timnah, he and his friend Hirah the Adullamite. And it was told Tamar, saying, "Look, your father-in-law is going up to Timnah to shear his sheep." So she took off her widow's garments, covered *herself* with a veil and wrapped herself, and sat in an open place which *was* on the way to Timnah; for she saw that Shelah was grown, and she was not given to him as a wife. When Judah saw her, he thought she *was* a harlot, because she had covered her face. Then he turned to her by the way, and said, "Please let me come in to you"; for he did not know that she *was* his daughter-in-law.

So she said, "What will you give me, that you may come in to me?" And he said, "I will send a young goat from the flock." So she said, "Will you give *me* a pledge till you send *it?*" Then he said, "What pledge shall I give you?" So she said, "Your signet and cord, and your staff that *is* in your hand." Then he gave *them* to her, and went in to her, and she conceived by him. So, she arose and went away, and laid aside her veil and put on the garments of her widowhood.

And Judah sent the young goat by the hand of his friend the Adullamite, to receive *his* pledge from the woman's hand, but he did not find her. Then he asked the men of that place, saying, "Where is the harlot who *was* openly by the roadside?" And they said, "There was no harlot in this *place.*" So he returned to Judah and said, "I cannot find her. Also, the men of the place said there was no harlot in this *place.*" Then Judah said, "Let her take *them* for herself, lest we be shamed; for I sent this young goat and you have not found her." And it came to pass, about three months after, that Judah was told, saying, "Tamar your daughter-in-law has played the harlot; furthermore, she *is* with child by harlotry." So Judah said, "Bring her out and let her be burned!" When she *was* brought out, she sent to her father-in-law, saying, "By the man to whom these belong, I *am* with child." And she said, "Please determine whose these *are*—the signet and cord, and staff." So Judah acknowledged *them* and said, "She has been more righteous than I, because I did not give her to Shelah my son." And he never knew her again.

Discussion Questions

1. How would you describe the relationship between Judah and his daughter-in-law?
2. What unhealthy patterns were present in this in-law relationship?
3. What can you learn from this passage about how to interact with in-laws?
4. What do you think about the way Tamar handled the situation?
5. Read Genesis 38:27-30, Ruth 4:18-22, and Matthew 1:1-6. How did this in-law relationship impact the relationship between God and mankind?
6. How do you see the hand of the Lord in your relationships with your in-laws and in your family line?

Exercise #4

Scenario #4: Examining 21st Century Family Life

Read the following scenario and answer the questions below.

Dean* and Samantha* have been married for three years. They have a three-month-old son. The couple dealt with infertility issues and a miscarriage since the beginning of their marriage. Finally, Dean and Samantha had a son. Samantha loved him so much. She was like Hannah, Sarah, and Leah; God heard her cry and blessed her womb to conceive. Samantha, affectionately called Sammie by her parents, got tired of getting up during the night to feed and change their son. Her solution: allow the baby to sleep in their bed. Dean moved to the living room couch or sometimes he slept on the floor beside the bed. Intimacy became a covert action as they snuck away to the living room couch and their son took over the bed. Sammie saw nothing wrong with this arrangement. Dean felt like a second-class citizen as he watched his son take his place.

He was close to his mother. He talked with her often about what was going on. She advised him to discuss these matters with his wife. When she came over to visit them, Dean's mother let a question slip about if the baby ever slept in his crib. Sammie became offended and told her mother-in-law that it was none of her business if he did or not. Dean didn't appreciate Sammie talking to his mother any kind of way. He berated and belittled her in front of his mother. Dean even got into her face as the argument escalated. He told her she will never disrespect his mother like that anymore. Sammie felt threatened by his behavior. Later that night, she called her mom and told her about it. Her mom advised her to come home and let her family take care of her. Sammie considered it that night and called her girlfriends for their opinions as Dean settled on the living room floor for another uncomfortable night of sleep.
*=fictitious names and situation

Discussion   Questions

1. How would you describe the family life in this scenario?
2. What unhealthy patterns are present in this scenario?
3. What healthy patterns need to be in place? What Biblical principles about marriage, children, and family should be applied?
4. What can you learn from this scenario regarding your own family life?
5. What could Dean and Samantha have done differently?

Exercise #5
Writing Prompts

Declaring Order and Decreeing Peace

In 1 Corinthians 14:40 NJKV, Paul advises the church at Corinth that when they are operating in their spiritual gifts during corporate worship, all things should be done decently and in order. We as a couple and a family are a corporate body within the body of Christ. Everything in our marriage and family life should be done decently and in order as well.

Earlier in the same chapter in verse 33, Paul states that God is not a God of confusion, but of peace. When we have unhealthy patterns in our parenting styles and our relationships with our in-laws, we will undoubtedly have confusion. Confusion leads to disagreement. Disagreement leads to discouragement and offense. Discouragement and offense lead to disorder and dissension. Disorder and dissension lead to no common ground in our marriage and possible separation between us as husband and wife.

We must declare order and decree peace. In this exercise, reflect on your responses and discussion of Exercises 1-4. What needs to be done decently and in order regarding your parenting and your in-laws? How can you bring clarity into these relationships and your family life? How can you bring peace in your family life? What is your vision for an ideal, healthier family life? Write your responses below.

Our Reflections

_____

_____

_____

_____

_____

_____

_____

_____

_____

_____

_____

_____

_____

Exercise #6

Putting Concept into Action

1. **Destructive Patterns/Thoughts:** Think about the unhealthy patterns present in your parenting style. Don't focus only on issues where you feel your spouse needs to be more involved or how your spouse makes your child more or less of a priority. Reflect on how each of you handles the kids. Think about unhealthy patterns present in your in-law relationships. Where do boundaries need to be redefined? Go back to your responses to the previous exercises. Now list 5 issues to work on.

   A. _____

   B. _____

   C. _____

   D. _____

   E. _____

2. **Divine Patterns/Thoughts:** What would be the Biblical response to those 5 things that you have listed? How can you respond in a healthy way?

   A._____
   _____
   _____

   B._____
   _____
   _____

   C._____
   _____
   _____

   D._____
   _____
   _____

   E. _____
   _____
   _____

3. **Developing Strategies:** Think of 3 actions that you can do to incorporate healthy, divine patterns into your relationship regarding this concern.

A._____

      1._____

      2._____

      3._____

B._____

      1._____

      2._____

      3._____

C._____

      1._____

      2._____

      3._____

D._____

      1._____

      2._____

      3._____

E._____

      1._____

      2._____

      3._____

Chapter 6 Writing Reflection
Creating Our Family Life Contract

Take this time to reflect on your responses to the exercises. For the writing reflection, you are going to create a family life contract. In classrooms, a teacher devises a behavioral contract with any students that have discipline or academic problems in the classroom. In this contract, the teacher identifies a plan of action to create the ideal behavioral or academic performance that draws out the student's potential. The teacher lists his or her role and responsibilities, and the student does the same. Then they write a plan of action to address what happens if the student failed to do his or her part. Afterwards, the teacher and student sign the contract and review it during the school year.

This is how you will write your family life contract. Use the paper provided to write it out. You may even want to type it and print it out.

Our Family Life Contract

- Our Family Life Mission Statement
- Our Family Life Vision
- Our Family Life Goals
- My Role and Responsibilities as a Husband & Father
  (regarding parenting, in-law relationships, and changed perspective of my wife)
- My Role and Responsibilities as a Wife & Mother
  (regarding parenting, in-law relationships, and changed perspective of my husband)
- Action Plans Concerns Regarding Parenting and In-Laws
- Dates to Reflect, Review, Redirect, and Revise

Our Family Life Contract

_____

_____

_____

_____

_____

_____

_____

Chapter 7

Our Intimacy

Intimacy can be defined as a total access of the soul; sharing of the sacred space of the heart. It can be physical, mental, emotional, and spiritual in nature. Intimacy is one of the major cornerstones of our marriages. If it is lacking or nonexistent, then the strength of the marriage is in trouble. There are many components that make up our intimacy. We have already discussed having an open communication. Another component is our sex lives. Sexual intimacy is very important in our marriages. It is a means of bonding as one flesh as well as expressing affection. Our needs play an intricate part in our sex life. If those needs are not being met, then that connection is lost.

Trust is another major cornerstone of our intimacy. The slightest suggestion of mistrust, even if it is one small omission of a detail, can negatively impact our closeness with each other. We must maintain openness, transparency, and honesty with each other. We also must be wise as serpents and harmless as doves, forever resistant to but not ignorant of the enemy's devices. The snares that can destroy our trust is our online communication, or what we refer to as Delilah's lap.

When we feel like our needs are not being met or when we experience frustration with our spouses, we must be careful to avoid making our social media accounts or our cell phones as a technological shoulder to cry on. The strange woman and the cunning man are out there to entice, ensnare, entrap, and bait us into adulterous liaisons that will wreck our marriages, our families, and our future generations.

Holding grudges, harboring unforgiveness, and having constant conflicts can affect our intimacy. They can bring confusion and open a door that leads to one of us seeking emotional comfort outside of the marriage. When we have these grievances or offenses, they are often accompanied by that look or attitude that cuts deeper than any blade can. Our homes become battlegrounds instead of safe havens of peace.

If we have no peace in our living space, then we do not have any peace within ourselves. As we fight with each other, we begin to lose a sense of self and forget why we even fell in love or got married. Now we are on a slippery slope, and we need course correction quickly before our intimacy is not the only thing that we have lost.

It is so important to maintain a common ground in our intimacy. Peace and conflict resolution are key to this maintenance. Exercising mercy and forgiveness are another set of keys needed to compromise and reconnect intimately. We must have the heart of God as we interact with each other in our marriages. If He says that we have all fallen short of the glory of God and He still pursues us with an everlasting love, then what makes us think we shouldn't do the same with each other?

It is time for us to rediscover who we were when we first met each other and fell in love. We need to forget about the socks on the floor, along with their minor irritations, and choose the path of peace. These final set of exercises will address unhealthy patterns that threaten to undermine our intimacy and equip us with strategies to reignite the flame and keep the peace.

Chapter 7 Objectives

- Gain revelation and understanding about your current view of intimacy
- Understand what peace, mercy, and forgiveness mean
- Learn about healthy patterns and perspectives regarding your intimacy as husband and wife
- Encourage open dialogue and improve communication between you and your spouse
- Learn strategies for reigniting the flame and resolving conflicts in a healthy way
- Commit to grow in learning more about your intimacy and the power of prayer

Negative Patterns Addressed in This Chapter

- From *Stop the Foolishness for Husbands*
    - Sex in the City
    - Find the Girl
    - Delilah's Lap: The Lure of Adultery
    - Illegitimate Peace
    - Forgiveness

- From *Stop the Foolishness for Wives*
    - Not Tonight, Dear
    - I'm Not Into What He's Into
    - Social Media Trap
    - Minefield
    - Concealed Weapon
    - The 'Tude
    - The Look
    - The Socks Are on the Floor Again

Exercise #1
Assessing What We Think About Our Intimacy

For this assessment, you are going to do something different. Take some quiet time to yourselves. Write a letter to each other in which you are open, honest, and transparent about your physical/sexual, emotional, mental, and spiritual intimacy. Include your thoughts about conflicts and how you feel like each other may have changed. Tell your spouse what you think about the current state of your intimacy. Afterwards, exchange letters and read them. Then write a letter to your spouse as a response, ask what he or she needs from you, and offer ways you can make things better. After you read the response letters, write your reflections on this exercise below.

Note: Write your letters on your own paper. You may want to do it electronically or on special stationery. You are going to write your reflections on the exercise after all the letters have been written and read.

Our Reflections

_____

_____

_____

_____

_____

_____

_____

_____

_____

_____

_____

_____

Exercise #2

Scenario #1: Love Lessons from Song of Solomon
(Song of Solomon 2:1-8, 16 NKJV)

Read the following verses and answer the questions below.

[Her Beloved]

Behold, you *are* fair, my love!
Behold, you *are* fair!
You *have* dove's eyes behind your veil.
Your hair *is* like a flock of goats,
Going down from Mount Gilead.
Your teeth *are* like a flock of shorn *sheep*
Which have come up from the washing,
Every one of which bears twins,
And none *is* barren among them.
Your lips *are* like a strand of scarlet,
And your mouth is lovely.
Your temples behind your veil
Are like a piece of pomegranate.

Your neck *is* like the tower of David,
Built for an armory,
On which hang a thousand bucklers,
All shields of mighty men.
Your two breasts *are* like two fawns,
Twins of a gazelle,
Which feed among the lilies.

Until the day breaks
And the shadows flee away,
I will go my way to the mountain of myrrh
And to the hill of frankincense.

You *are* all fair, my love,
And *there is* no spot in you.
Come with me from Lebanon, *my* spouse,
With me from Lebanon.
Look from the top of Amana,
From the top of Senir and Hermon,
From the lions' dens,
From the mountains of the leopards.

[Shulamite Woman]

Awake, O north *wind,*
And come, O south!
Blow upon my garden,
That its spices may flow out.
Let my beloved come to his garden
And eat its pleasant fruits.

Discussion Questions

1. Describe the intimacy between the husband and wife in these verses.
2. What healthy patterns are present in their communication? Are there any negative patterns?
3. What can you learn from this example that you can apply to your intimacy?
4. Tell your spouse of his or her attributes like King Solomon and the Shulamite bride.

Exercise #3

Scenario #2: What about Forever Holding Our Marital Peace?

Read the following verses and answer the questions below.

"Be still, and know that I am God. I will be exalted among the nations; I will be exalted in the earth!" (Psalms 46:10 ESV)

"Agree with God, and be at peace; thereby good will come to you." (Job 22:21 ESV)

"Blessed [spiritually calm with life-joy in God's favor] are the makers *and* maintainers of peace, for they will [express His character and] be called the sons of God. "Blessed [comforted by inner peace and God's love] are those who are persecuted for doing that which is morally right, for theirs is the kingdom of heaven [both now and forever]. (Matthew 5:9-10 AMP)

Discussion Questions

1. How does the Bible define peace? What should peace look like in a marriage?
2. What is a peacemaker?
3. How can you be a peacemaker in your marriage?
4. What can threaten your marital peace?
5. What is currently threatening your marital peace?

Exercise #4

Scenario #3: Mercy & Forgiveness (Luke 15:13-32 NKJV)

Read the following verses and answer the questions below.

 And not many days after, the younger son gathered all together, journeyed to a far country, and there wasted his possessions with prodigal living. But when he had spent all, there arose a severe famine in that land, and he began to be in want. Then he went and joined himself to a citizen of that country, and he sent him into his fields to feed swine. And he would gladly have filled his stomach with the ᴵpods that the swine ate, and no one gave him *anything*.

"But when he came to himself, he said, 'How many of my father's hired servants have bread enough and to spare, and I perish with hunger! I will arise and go to my father, and will say to him, "Father, I have sinned against heaven and before you, and I am no longer worthy to be called your son. Make me like one of your hired servants."'

"And he arose and came to his father. But when he was still a great way off, his father saw him and had compassion, and ran and fell on his neck and kissed him. And the son said to him, 'Father, I have sinned against heaven and in your sight, and am no longer worthy to be called your son.'

"But the father said to his servants, 'Bring out the best robe and put *it* on him, and put a ring on his hand and sandals on *his* feet. And bring the fatted calf here and kill *it,* and let us eat and be merry; for this my son was dead and is alive again; he was lost and is found.' And they began to be merry.

"Now his older son was in the field. And as he came and drew near to the house, he heard music and dancing. So he called one of the servants and asked what these things meant. And he said to him, 'Your brother has come, and because he has received him safe and sound, your father has killed the fatted calf.'

"But he was angry and would not go in. Therefore, his father came out and pleaded with him. So he answered and said to *his* father, 'Lo, these many years I have been serving you; I never transgressed your commandment at any time; and yet you never gave me a young goat that I might make merry with my friends. But as soon as this son of yours came, who has devoured your livelihood with harlots, you killed the fatted calf for him.'

"And he said to him, 'Son, you are always with me, and all that I have is yours. It was right that we should make merry and be glad, for your brother was dead and is alive again, and was lost and is found.'"

Discussion Questions

1. What healthy and unhealthy patterns do you see in this parable?
2. How would you define mercy? How is it present in your marriage?
3. How would you define forgiveness? How is it present in your marriage?
4. What principles from the parable can you apply to your marriage to improve your intimacy?

Exercise #5
Writing Prompts

Finding the Star-Crossed Lovers Again

In Matthew 13:24-30 NJKV, Jesus tells the parable of the wheat and the tares to explain a kingdom principle. The parable can also be applied to our intimacy. When we started this marriage, we sowed good seeds of love, intimacy, friendship, and connection. We were each other's peace, a serene place where we could be ourselves with each other and be at peace. We romanced each other all the time, calling and texting like adolescents while grinning from ear to ear.

Then something happened. As our marriage progressed, children entered our lives and lives have changed. The enemy started sowing those tares. It started out like little foxes on the vine, or socks on the floor again, or petty grievances. Such a distance has grown in our intimacy that results in losing a piece of us relationally and individually. How did we get here? How can we find the girl again? How can we find the star-crossed young man?

Reflect and discuss with your spouse. What tares have been sown into your emotional, physical/sexual, mental, or spiritual intimacy? How can you uproot those tares and regain that star-crossed love again? How can you spice up your romantic life? Write your reflections below.

Our Reflections

_____

_____

_____

_____

_____

_____

_____

_____

_____

_____

_____

_____

Exercise #6
The ABCs of Conflict Resolution

In *Stop the Foolishness for Wives*, Fiona introduced a strategy called the A-B-C Principle. It was an approach for complaining without criticizing or showing contempt. We would like to adapt this strategy as a model for conflict resolution. Think about what you have complained about in your marriage. What are some statements that you have made that could be labeled as criticism or contempt? (Fiona gave some excellent examples in her book.)

In her strategy, she asked you to state the action, how you feel, and what you would like changed or what you need. We are going to add another C to this strategy: what common ground or compromise can you reach with your spouse (how can you initiate and maintain peace)?

Complete the exercise below.

A-B-C² Strategy

Conflict #1:

A – State the **Action**: _____

B – **Be** honest in how you feel: _____

_____

_____

C – **Changes** you want to make or needs you want to have met:

1. _____

2. _____

3. _____

4. _____

C² – Our **Common Ground** or **Compromise**

_____

_____

_____

Conflict #2:

A – State the **Action**: _____

B – **Be** honest in how you feel: _____

_____

_____

C – **Changes** you want to make or needs you want to have met:

1. _____

2. _____

3. _____

4. _____

C² – Our **Common Ground** or **Compromise**

_____

_____

_____

_____

Conflict #3:

A – State the **Action**: _____

B – **Be** honest in how you feel: _____

_____

_____

C – Changes you want to make or needs you want to have met:

1. _____
2. _____
3. _____
4. _____

C² – Our **Common Ground** or **Compromise**

_____

_____

_____

_____

_____

Conflict #4:

A – State the **Action**: _____

B – Be honest in how you feel: _____

_____

_____

C – Changes you want to make or needs you want to have met:

1. _____
2. _____
3. _____
4. _____

C² – Our **Common Ground** or **Compromise**

_____

_____

_____

_____

C² – Our **Common Ground** or **Compromise**

Exercise #7
Making War in the Prayer Room, Not Our Marriage

In 2015, Priscilla Shirer starred in the movie, *War Room*. In this movie, she played a wife who experienced marital problems. She met an elderly widow who taught her the power of prayer. Priscilla's character transformed her walk-in closet into a war room. She wrote prayers concerning her marriage and attached them to the walls. Her character would write down when God answered her prayers, and she went in the room daily to make intercession for her marriage and family. Then the wife took it a strategic step further. She regained control of her atmosphere and cast the enemy out of her house. As the movie progressed, the husband refused to engage in Delilah's trap and went home to his wife. Prayer changes things. The grudge, unforgiveness, lack of sexual intimacy, or the conflicts are distractions from the enemy. We react to the cut instead of responding with a solution of healing and reconciliation.

Your assignment is one that will not take place in the workbook. You will create your own war room. It can be your own walk-in closet or a section of a room in your home. You can cut string or yarn, tape it behind a closet door, purchase some clothespins, and attach prayers on slips of paper or index cards. You decide how and where you will post your prayers. Date them when God answers them, and even record how He answered them. War for your marriage. Each grudge, every argument, every unforgiveness that you have, write a prayer in which you intercede for the solution. When you feel like giving your spouse an attitude, a curt remark, or a look, write a prayer interceding for him or her. Pray for his job, his health, his mind, her family, her finances, her heart, or her parents. Live out Matthew 5:44. Speak and pray blessings, do something good, and spread love and peace.

Will you accept the challenge and make war in your prayer room instead of your marriage?

Exercise #8
Putting Concept into Action

1. **Destructive Patterns/Thoughts:** Think about the unhealthy patterns present in your intimacy. What grudges have you been holding? What makes you give your spouse a look or an attitude? What unforgiveness have you been harboring? What kinds of seeds have you been sowing into your intimacy? What seeds have been stealing peace from your intimacy? What unhealthy patterns are in your sex life? List 5 issues or concerns that you want to address.

    A. _____

    B. _____

    C. _____

    D. _____

    E. _____

2. **Divine Patterns/Thoughts:** What would be the Biblical response to those 5 things that you have listed? How can you respond in a healthy way?

    A. _____

    _____

    _____

    B. _____

    _____

    _____

    C. _____

    _____

    _____

    D. _____

    _____

    _____

E. _____

_____

_____

3. Developing Strategies: Think of 3 actions that you can do to incorporate healthy, divine patterns into your relationship regarding this concern.

A. _____

    1. _____

    2. _____

    3. _____

B. _____

    1. _____

    2. _____

    3. _____

C. _____

    1. _____

    2. _____

    3. _____

D. _____

    1. _____

    2. _____

    3. _____

E. _____

    1. _____

    2. _____

    3. _____

Chapter 7 Writing Reflection
Creating Our Marital Goals

Take this time to reflect on your responses to the exercises from this chapter. You are going to write goals for your marriage and your intimacy. What do you want intimacy to look like in your marriage? How do you want to make your home a safe haven? How do you want to encourage more peace, forgiveness, and mercy in your marriage? What goals do you want to set for reigniting the flame and making time for each other? What goals do you want to set for your online communication? What other goals do you want to set for your intimacy? Once you write your goals, reflect on what action steps you need to take to accomplish them. Afterwards, write a prayer to God about your intimacy. Use the space below.

Our Goals

STOP THE FOOLISHNESS FOR COUPLES

168

Our Action Steps

Our Prayer for Our Intimacy

Final Assignments
Our Future Journey in the Lord
(Our Marriage Affirmations, Our Love Letters, & Our Prayer for Our Marriage)

As you move forward, continue to walk in your journey with the Lord. Just like He is the Lord of the harvest of lost and prodigal souls, He is the Lord of your marriage. For His word is true: what He has brought together, let no man put asunder. You have learned the unhealthy patterns that can negatively impact your marriage. Now you know how to debunk those negative systems of thoughts, actions, and emotions and replace them with healthy, divine patterns that sustain your marriage. Your final assignments are to write affirmations, love letters, and a prayer for your marriage.

Marriage affirmations are positive statements that you declare and decree over your marriage. God the Creator is inside of you. He spoke into a dark and void earth and declared, "Let there be light." And there was light. His words created everything He wanted to see in the earth, and it manifested into existence. The world, the enemy, and even the enemy of your flesh may be declaring what your marriage is or who your spouse is, but they do not have the final say in your marriage. The One who said let no man put it asunder, The One who said My word will not return unto Me void and promises to perform it, the great I Am That I Am declared and decreed that your marriage shall live and not die and declare His glory. Speak into existence what you want to see in your marriage and your spouse. Speak the word over your marriage, your spouse, and your family. Fight for it in the Spirit.

Love letters to each other are the second assignment. Your journey now comes full circle by writing love letters to rededicate yourselves, your love, and your commitment to each other. During this journey, you have been honest, vulnerable, transparent, and willing to do the work to draw closer to each in God. Remember Paul stated in 2 Corinthians 3:2-3 KJV that we are living epistles. We love each other like Christ loved us. When we write, our words become a permanent living epistle, a vision that we can run with on those challenging days in our marriages.

Prayer is the last assignment. It should remain a vital part of your daily devotional lives. Pray to the Lord over the future of your marriage. Ask Him to give you and your spouse the wisdom, understanding, strength, patience, and grace to move forward and to continue to stop the foolishness in your marriage.

Use the following pages to complete these final three assignments.

OUR MARRIAGE AFFIRMATIONS

1. _____
2. _____
3. _____
4. _____
5. _____
6. _____
7. _____
8. _____

Love Letter to My Husband

Love Letter to My Wife

_____

_____

_____

_____

_____

_____

_____

_____

_____

_____

_____

_____

_____

_____

_____

_____

_____

_____

_____

_____

_____

_____

_____

_____

_____

_____

_____

_____

_____

Our Prayer for Our Marriage